COOKING WITH
MOSIMANN

Anton Mosimann was born in 1947 at Solothurn, Switzerland. A fourth-generation chef, he first decided to follow the profession at the age of six. He trained and worked in Italy, Canada, Belgium, France and Japan, as well as in his native Switzerland. In 1976, at the age of only twenty-eight, he was appointed Maître-chef des Cuisines at The Dorchester Hotel in London. His skills, energy and innovation brought accolades on the hotel's two restaurants, as well as two stars in the *Guide Michelin*. In 1988 Anton Mosimann left The Dorchester and established Mosimann's, a restaurant-club in Belgravia.

Anton Mosimann's first book, *Cuisine à la Carte*, was acclaimed as 'a must for unrepentant gourmets' by Prue Leith in her *Guardian* review. It was followed by his innovatory *Cuisine Naturelle*, a collection of recipes capturing the essential taste, integrity and nutritional value of the ingredients to enable his followers to eat healthily. *Fish Cuisine* was published in 1988 and was described by *The Sunday Times* as 'an exceptionally beautiful book, informative, well-presented and most important, full of scrumptious recipes'.

Mosimann is a frequent broadcaster and has made notable television programmes, cooking in a council house in Sheffield and contributing as chef to *The BBC Diet*. *Cooking with Mosimann* is his first major television series.

Also by Anton Mosimann

Cuisine à la Carte
Cuisine Naturelle
Fish Cuisine
A New Style of Cooking

COOKING WITH MOSIMANN

ANTON MOSIMANN

PAPERMAC

in association with Channel Four Television Company Limited
and Yorkshire Television Limited

To Kit Chan

First published in the United Kingdom 1989 by
PAPERMAC
a division of Pan Macmillan Publishers Limited
Cavaye Place London SW10 9PG
and Basingstoke

Reprinted 1990, 1991, 1992, 1994

Associated companies in Auckland, Budapest, Dublin, Gaborone,
Harare, Hong Kong, Kampala, Kuala Lumpur, Lagos, Madras,
Manzini, Melbourne, Mexico City, Nairobi, New York, Singapore,
Sydney, Tokyo and Windhoek

A CIP catalogue record for this book is available from
the British Library.

ISBN 0-333-51187-5

Design by Geoff Hayes
Food photography by Tom Belshaw
Location photography copyright YTV
Line Illustrations by Soun Vannithone
Tableware by Divertimenti and Wedgwood

Typeset by Rowland Phototypesetting Limted, Bury St Edmunds, Suffolk
Printed in Hong Kong

CONTENTS

Acknowledgements

I want to thank particularly David Wilson, Director, and Melanie Davis, Associate Producer, of Yorkshire Television for the tremendous amount of effort they put into the series accompanying this book. It was wonderful working with them both, and feeling we have created something worthwhile. I would also like to thank Susan Fleming, my editor, who has worked with me on my recent books and to whom I am indebted, and Katrina Whone for all her help and support. My thanks also to Lyn Hall, of La Petite Cuisine, my Restaurant Manager, John Davey, and his staff, Ralph Bürgin, Head Chef at my club and his Kitchen Brigade, and most particularly Kit Chan. My thanks also to Tom Belshaw, photographer, ever even-tempered when I so often change my mind, and last, but certainly not least, my secretary Valerie Shields.

INTRODUCTION

Cooking is a fascinating profession. To be *good* at cooking, a chef needs to be totally dedicated to his work; he must also love it, and needs to be the eternal apprentice, forever questioning, experimenting, discovering and adapting. I myself constantly seek fresh experience, expertise and skills, and hope I shall never be too old to learn something new! But cooking is also fascinating for the non-professional, for all those who enjoy reading a cookbook as much as the latest bestseller, who enjoy recreating and experimenting with other cooks' recipes, and who have that same commitment to and enthusiasm for good food.

Most chefs undergo a quite arduous training, ranging over several years of basic tuition, and covering many individual disciplines. He or she needs to understand and be able to apply the absolute basics of 'cooking' – the various ways of preparing and transforming raw food ingredients into appetising dishes – for without these, the foundation stones of the art, there can be no way in which one can progress. However, he or she must also know, and know how to apply that knowledge, of the nature and properties of food, the 'chemistry', the economics, and the aesthetics of food, and these too require dedication and an intellectual as well as emotional commitment. Such extensive expertise is not easy for the non-professional to acquire, but the same basic principles are just as important and relevant in the home kitchen as in the restaurant kitchen.

This is why in this book, and in the television series which it accompanies, I have approached cooking in a way that is easily adaptable to home use. I have explored different kinds of meals, different ways of shopping, and different modes of eating. I have interspersed chapters and recipes with tips which will go some way towards explaining the whys and wherefores of ingredients and techniques, and some of the more seemingly esoteric aspects of *my* cooking. It is not intended to be a textbook, however – although teaching my art to others is something I enjoy very much – but it should bring the reader closer to the versatility of many of the ideas that I consider central to my cooking and to my culinary philosophies.

A desire for perfection is one of the qualities I believe vital in a good chef, and there is no reason why the home cook should not aspire to that as well. A major facet of this quest for perfection is buying the best and freshest ingredients, and this is always possible now, when top-quality produce is available, in specialist shops and markets as well as supermarkets, from all over the world, and at all times of the year. And buying in season makes good economic sense as well, both for the professional and for the home cook. Whatever produce is best that day – of vegetables, fruit, meat and fish – should determine the individual dishes and the menu as a whole. I believe wholeheartedly that any cook, whether professional or not, must spend time, daily if at all possible, examining the fresh produce on offer, and then buy accordingly. No one should ever go shopping with a fixed idea, with a particular recipe or menu in mind, for shopping should be spontaneous in a sense, with the ingredients themselves inspiring ideas of how to use them and with what. It may be less easy at first for the home cook to recognise that the freshest and best fish available today can be cooked in much the same way as another favourite fish recipe cooked yesterday – but this knowledge will come in time. The Menu Surprise, which I introduced at the Dorchester in 1978, was created on that very principle – serving what was best in the markets that day – and you will find a typical example of it in the dinner party chapter in this book.

Another aspect of the desire for perfection which I consider so essential, lies, of course, in the cooking of those top-quality ingredients. It should always be as simple and delicate as possible, so that the foods retain as much of their quintessential nature and individual flavour as possible. Many of these simpler and more delicate cooking techniques create a lighter, more natural result, and one which is also healthier – for health is very much a major concern of mine. Food that is light and wholesome, that is prepared carefully and with love, can truly contribute to health and to inner well-being. In 1985 I developed Cuisine Naturelle to demonstrate just that, how good food and food that is good for you can co-exist, can go hand in hand. In these days of anxiety over heart disease, overweight, and cholesterol, Cuisine Naturelle shows how to cut out or down on many of the ingredients thought to contribute to ill health, such as oil, butter, cream, alcohol, salt and sugar, but without diminishing the essential enjoyment of the dishes. Many of the recipes in this book were developed on these Cuisine Naturelle principles, and indeed I have presumed to approach two great British traditions – those of breakfast and Sunday lunch – from the standpoint of health, daring to suggest that there are ways in which dishes might be adapted, sometimes only marginally, to produce a healthier, but still uniquely delicious, result!

I love cooking, and it gives me infinite pleasure to make people happy with good food. This I do in my professional capacity every day of my life for guests at Mosimann's, the club that I opened in 1988. There, as I have always done in my many years of cooking, I continue to adapt my skills, to initiate fresh ideas, and seek to achieve the final culinary perfection to delight those for whom I recreate my art. I also love cooking for my family and for my friends at home, and like nothing better than to transform a holiday weekend with leisurely and healthy breakfasts, and picnics and barbecues in the open air. I need little excuse to celebrate – a sunny Sunday, an unexpected visit from an old friend, the arrival of the first English asparagus, new lamb from Wales or those delicious fresh sardines – and for all of us there's always a reason for celebration.

Whether you're planning the ultimate black-tie dinner, or a relaxing day of feasting in the garden, the selection of recipes here reflects what I consider my own creativity: some are very special indeed, and some are for simpler, although no less delicious, dishes which I like to cook at home. Whichever type of cooking or eating you prefer, I hope that you enjoy the recipes, for cooking them should give as much pleasure to the cook as to the guests. I also hope that you consider the book and the television series have succeeded in their aim – to share with you my culinary philosophies, my creativity, my versatility and, above all, my love of good food.

Anton Mosimann
London 1989

COOKING WITH
MOSIMANN

BREAKFAST

Having been the chef in many a wonderful hotel around the world, I gain particular pleasure from the sight of people sitting down to a good breakfast. Whether you're preparing yourself for the rigours of a chill and foggy day in England, with a good helping of kedgeree and plenty of brown buttered toast, or you're sitting on a sunny terrace in the mountains, contemplating a day's walking with a creamy banana cocktail and bowl of fruit muesli, breakfast gives a great sense of well being and makes a good start to the day.

For breakfast, I think, is one of the most important meals of the day. After at least ten hours of fasting, our bodies need fuel to get them going, rather like a car needs petrol! Most

Oat Muesli with Fruit (page 5)

2

people in our busy times tend to skimp on the meal, grabbing a cup of coffee or slice of toast, and think that will last them until lunchtime. But tests have shown conclusively that those who don't eat properly in the morning are less efficient, less productive and quite often are less even-tempered. School-children are thought to lack concentration too, so it is doubly important for them to start the day off well.

An old saying states that we should 'breakfast like a king, lunch like a prince, and dine like a pauper'. There's a lot of truth in this, as we don't need fuel for sleeping – if the body is busy digesting, it won't be resting. However, the king-sized breakfast traditionally enjoyed in England could be improved upon, I think.

Porridge or cereals, bacon, eggs, sausages and kippers are part of what has become known as the Great British Breakfast. It was the wealthier Victorians who really revolutionised breakfast eating: their sideboards groaned with chafing dishes full of eggs in all guises, kedgeree and other fish dishes, and devilled meats. Now traditional breakfasts are seen more as an indulgence, an occasional treat for once a week or month, at the weekend, for instance, or when travelling on a train. This was confirmed by conversations I had on the Leeds to London train one morning when filming for the series this book accompanies. I was still surprised, though, that out of sixty-five breakfasts served by the chef (from an extraordinarily small kitchen), forty of them (or sixty per cent) were traditional – porridge or cereal, eggs, bacon, sausages, fried bread, toast, marmalade, the lot! (This meal is also, apparently, the one which generates most of British Rail's business.)

So the British still seem to be very attached to their breakfasts, and it is not for me to try to overturn such a tradition. (Indeed I believe there was a national outcry after kippers disappeared from the breakfast menu of the Brighton to London train; Sir Laurence Olivier was moved to write a letter to *The Times* about it.) However, I venture to suggest that there are ways of making breakfasts quite a bit healthier. Yes, once a week have a 'traditional' meal, but serve a muesli or a fruit dish instead of manufactured cereal; have foods that are cooked in less oil and fat, like my fried egg and sausage. For the rest of the week, instead of over-indulging in protein, there is a wealth of dishes that can be put together or cooked quickly to give you the desired fuel. You may think you have no time, but there can be no hardship in going to bed a little earlier in order to have an extra ten minutes in the morning. By setting the table the evening before and preparing most of the ingredients, little encouragement is needed to rise those few minutes earlier to finish breakfast preparation – something nourishing like yoghurt with fruits, a fruit compôte or fruit drink, or my muesli. It's all a matter of organisation – and your working day and your working body will be all the better for it!

HOME-MADE FRUIT YOGHURT

Home-made yoghurt is quite delicious, and made with skimmed milk and low-fat yoghurt as here, it's less rich than bought. You can, of course, leave out the cream and sugar – it all depends on the sweetness of the fruits available and the flavour that you want.

Serves 4

500 ml (18 fl oz) skimmed milk	Bring to the boil, then cool down to blood heat, 37°C/98.6°F.
10 ml (2 tsp) low-fat plain yoghurt	Put into a wide-necked jar, pour the cooled milk over it and whisk vigorously. Cover the jar and transfer to a warm place overnight, or for a minimum of 6 hours. By then it will have thickened to a delicious natural yoghurt. Do not move the jar at any time, or the whey will separate, and make for a watery yoghurt. Cool in the refrigerator for a few hours, again not moving, then spoon into a wide bowl.
50 g (2 oz) sugar about **300 g** (11 oz) seasonal fruits (berries, apples, pears, etc)	Add sugar to taste and the fruit, washed, prepared and finely sliced as necessary.
50 ml (2 fl oz) whipping cream, whipped until stiff (optional)	Fold in and serve.

TIPS
All equipment should be rinsed clean, with no trace of detergent, which can interfere with the set.
    30 ml (2 tbsp) skimmed milk powder added to the yoghurt gives a (harmless) richness; so does simmering it very slowly, without allowing it to bubble, and reducing it by one-third before cooling it to blood heat.
    Use your own home-made yoghurt to start off the next batch as soon as possible: your yoghurt will become better and better.

OAT MUESLI WITH FRUIT

A delicious way to start a healthy breakfast. It is an adaptation of the famous Swiss muesli, using oats only. You can, of course, vary the cereal content, but the texture must always be soft and creamy, so you may need more milk and yoghurt. Vary fruits according to season. If you soak the oats overnight in a cool place the milk need not be warmed.

Serves 4

60 ml (4 tbsp) rolled oats **15 ml** (1 tbsp) oat germ and bran **100 ml** (4 fl oz) skimmed milk, warmed	Soak together for at least 2 hours in a bowl.
150 g (5 oz) plain yoghurt **60 ml** (4 tbsp) honey **30 ml** (2 tbsp) lemon juice	Stir in, and mix together.
2 apples, 1 red and 1 green, washed and cored, grated (with skin) **60 ml** (4 tbsp) hazelnuts, toasted, skinned and chopped	Add to the mixture.
300 g (11 oz) berries (strawberries, raspberries, currants, blueberries, blackberries etc)	Slice if necessary, and fold in just before serving.
4 sprigs fresh mint **4–8 whole** berries in perfect condition	Garnish and serve.

EXOTIC FRESH FRUIT PLATTER

Fresh fruit makes a very healthy breakfast – it's satisfying and full of fibre and other goodness.

Serves 4

1 papaya, peeled	Cut in half, and remove the seeds.
1 mango, peeled	Cut the flesh away from the large flat central stone.
2 kiwi fruit, peeled	Slice the flesh of the kiwi, papaya and mango.
2 oranges, segmented **4** large strawberries, sliced **20** raspberries **8** fresh dates, halved and stoned **12** cherries	Arrange all the fruits decoratively on a platter, or individual plates.
4 sprigs fresh mint	Garnish and serve.

TIP
To segment an orange (or any citrus fruit), use a very sharp knife, and cut away all the skin and pith together (1) (2). Work over a bowl to catch the juices. Holding the peeled orange in your non-working hand, cut on either side of each segment, leaving behind the thin membrane. As your knife cuts towards the middle of the orange, the membrane-free segment will slip out (3). Squeeze the membrane core to extract the remaining juice (4).

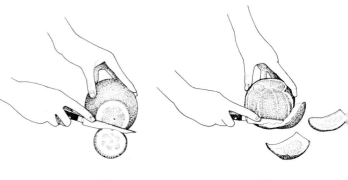

(1)

(2)

(3)

(4)

DRIED FRUIT COMPÔTE

TIP
To make the sugar syrup, place 350 g (12 oz) caster sugar in 1 litre (1¾ pints) water. Add the zest and juice of 1 lemon, the zest of a ½ orange, the juice of 1½ oranges, plus a cinnamon stick. Bring to the boil, and simmer for 3–4 minutes or until the sugar has dissolved. Allow to cool, then use as required.

You can use any dried fruit for this, or a mixture – apple rings, pears, peaches, prunes, raisins or apricots. It is important to have plenty of colour, shapes and sizes. The basis is a sugar syrup which can be used for many other fruit dishes. Cover the selected fruits with the strained syrup, and, if you like, you could also add a little rum. Leave to soak in a cool place at least overnight.

You could serve the compôte at breakfast by itself, or a little is also delicious served with yoghurt, ice-cream or bread and butter pudding.

OMELETTE

A properly prepared omelette should be moist and creamy inside, not firm or overcooked. Garnishes and fillings can be added in various ways, see below – there are many from which to choose.

Serves 1

3 eggs a pinch of salt	Whisk together lightly in a bowl.
15 g (½ oz) butter	Melt in an omelette or non-stick pan, and strain in the eggs. Return to a brisk heat. The mixture should begin to cook immediately at the outer edges. Lift the firm edges so the liquid egg can flow out from underneath. Slide pan rapidly back and forth over heat to keep the omelette in motion, and to avoid sticking. The mixture is done when liquid egg ceases to flow from beneath it. Tip the pan to help you fold it over into a neat oval in the front of the pan, and turn on to a warm plate.

Variations

Fines Herbes	Add 15 ml (1 tbsp) finely chopped fresh herbs (parsley, chives, chervil, tarragon) to the beaten eggs before cooking.
Cheese	Grate 50 g (2 oz) good cheese (Emmental, Gruyère, Cheddar), and add half to the beaten eggs before cooking. Sprinkle the remainder on the omelette before folding.
Tomato or Mushroom	Soften 2 skinned, seasoned and diced tomatoes or 50 g (2 oz) sliced mushrooms (cultivated or wild) in a little butter. Spoon on to the omelette before folding over.
Smoked Salmon and Chives	Cut about 50 g (2 oz) smoked salmon and place on the omelette, with about 15 ml (1 tbsp) snipped chives, before folding.
Smoked Haddock	Add about 50 g (2 oz) creamy cooked and flaked smoked haddock before folding the omelette.
Chicken Livers or Smoked Chicken	Grill some chicken livers (or fry in a little butter). Or finely slice some smoked chicken and warm through slightly. Cut into the centre of the omelette oval, pull cut apart a little and place livers or chicken on top.

TIP

An omelette pan of thin, lined copper is ideal: it conducts the heat swiftly, thereby allowing the omelette to cook rapidly to a light golden crust outside, while remaining creamy and moist inside. It also loses heat quickly when it is taken from the heat, preventing the omelette from overcooking.

VEAL AND SPINACH SAUSAGE

There is a saying that only two people know the ingredients of a sausage – the butcher who made it, and God. That's sad, I think, because sausages are such a simple and basic concept, and *can* be so good without the unnecessary breadcrumbs, starch etc. I like them very much at breakfast, and this way of cooking them – poaching first to cook, then grilling to colour – is very much healthier. You could make chicken, meat, fish or vegetable sausages too, in exactly the same way.

Makes 10

50 g (2 oz) onion, finely chopped **10 ml** (2 tsp) olive oil	In a pan, sweat the onion in the oil to soften, not colour, and then leave to cool.
300 g (11 oz) lean shoulder of veal, diced	Pass through a fine mincer twice and keep cold in a basin over a bowl of ice.
100 g (4 oz) fresh spinach, blanched and finely chopped	To achieve a fine texture, put the veal, onion and spinach in a food processor and process for a few seconds.
1 egg **50 g** (2 oz) fromage blanc or quark (see pages 200 and 201) **15 ml** (1 tbsp) each chopped parsley and chopped sage	Add to the mixture. (You have to work fairly quickly to make sure the mixture doesn't get too warm.)
salt, freshly ground pepper and freshly grated nutmeg	Season the mixture to taste.
sausage casings, pre-soaked	Rest the mixture for about an hour in the refrigerator, then pipe the mixture into the sausage casing – not too full, as they expand – using a piping bag. Twist and tie at intervals to the desired length, approximately 10 cm (4 in). Knot at the ends. Poach in hot water (not boiling) for 5 minutes, then drain, refresh in cold water, and cool. Place under a grill or on a fat-free grill surface or hot-plate for 4–5 minutes to colour. Serve with grilled tomatoes (yellow as well as red for colour), grilled flat mushrooms and Mosimann's fried egg.

TIP

Home-made sausages are very much easier to make than you might think, and you don't need any special equipment. You must have sausage casings though, and these you can get from your butcher. Soak them in salted water overnight to make them flexible.

Clockwise: Kedgeree (page 13);
Breakfast Cocktail (page 29);
Mosimann's Fried Egg (right); Veal
and Spinach Sausage (opposite)

MOSIMANN'S FRIED EGG

Fried eggs are very much part of the traditional British breakfast, but they are generally cooked in too much fat. This is my solution.

You must use eggs that are very fresh. Simply place the serving plate over a pan of simmering water, and allow the plate to become hot. Crack the egg straight on to the hot plate, and it will immediately start to set. Cover with a cloche or lid – another inverted plate will do – and cook for 3–4 minutes, or until done to your taste. Season to taste. It takes a little longer than a conventional fried egg.

SCRAMBLED EGGS

Softly scrambled eggs are excellent on their own, served on hot brown toast and sprinkled with fresh herbs, particularly chives, or a dusting of paprika. They also go well with other breakfast favourites like grilled bacon and tomatoes, and with kippers (a traditional northern combination). For a special occasion, garnish with a few slivers of smoked salmon or smoked haddock.

Serves 1

15 g (½ oz) butter	Melt in a sauté pan.
2 large eggs, mixed well with a fork	Strain into the pan, and stir into a thick moist mass, using a wooden spoon and a very low temperature.
salt and freshly ground pepper	Season to taste just before serving.
15 ml (1 tbsp) cream (optional)	Stir in if using. The eggs should look soft and creamy.

DEVILLED KIDNEYS

Breakfast in Victorian and Edwardian times was a substantial affair. The devilled sauce – a spiced mixture for meat – became especially popular with kidneys, although lamb cutlets or thick slices of roast mutton were also devilled for breakfast.

Serves 4

15 ml (1 tbsp) plain or wholemeal flour salt cayenne pepper 15 ml (1 tbsp) dry mustard powder	Sift together on to a plate.
8 fresh lamb's kidneys, cleaned and cut into small cubes	Roll in the spiced flour.
50 g (2 oz) butter	Melt in a small frying pan and cook the kidneys over low heat for about 1 minute, turning them occasionally.
100 ml (4 fl oz) chicken stock (see page 193)	Pour over the kidneys, and simmer uncovered for about another minute, until the sauce thickens a little and the kidneys are done.
4 slices hot buttered wholemeal toast 4 sprigs parsley	Taste for seasoning, then divide between the slices of toast. Cut each slice in half diagonally and garnish.

KEDGEREE

Kedgeree is an Anglo-Indian adaptation of the original Hindi *khicharhi* or *khichri*, which consisted of rice, onion, lentils, spices, fresh limes, *ghee* and fish or meat. This is a simpler breakfast version, and is served with a mild, but interesting, curry sauce.

Serves 4	**Oven:** moderately hot, 190°C/375°F/Gas 5
300 ml (½ pint) fish stock (see page 195) or water **1** sprig parsley or thyme, or a few chives	Bring to the boil.
300 g (11 oz) smoked Finnan haddock with skin	Add and poach in barely simmering liquid for about 3–4 minutes. Remove the fish and leave to cool. Strain the stock and keep.
20 ml (4 tsp) olive oil **50 g** (2 oz) onion, finely chopped	Heat the oil in a suitable pan and soften the onion for a few minutes.
150 g (5 oz) basmati rice	Stir in, and mix well with the onion. When the rice starts to look transparent, add the fish stock, and bring to a simmer. Cover and cook in the oven for about 15–16 minutes, until the rice is tender and fluffy and has absorbed the stock. Meanwhile, skin, bone and flake the smoked haddock. (It doesn't matter if it is slightly undercooked at this stage; it will finish cooking when mixed with the hot rice.)
5 ml (1 tsp) chopped parsley salt and freshly ground pepper	Use a fork to separate and loosen the rice, then add the flaked haddock, parsley, and seasoning to taste.
8 quails' eggs, medium boiled and peeled (see page 172)	Serve the kedgeree in a warm dish or on individual plates, garnished with the eggs, on top of the following curry sauce.

TIP
Keep the skin on the fish while you're poaching it, as this keeps the flesh moister, giving a better result.

M

KEDGEREE CURRY SAUCE

This curry sauce, which imparts its spiciness to a breakfast kedgeree, would also be good with hard-boiled eggs, and cooked vegetables or meat (but use vegetable or chicken stock instead of fish).

Makes 300 ml (½ pint)

100 g (4 oz) onion, finely chopped
1 garlic clove, crushed
30 ml (2 tbsp) olive oil

Sweat the onion and garlic in the olive oil until soft.

50 g (2 oz) carrot, finely chopped
50 g (2 oz) celery, finely chopped
100 g (4 oz) apple, finely chopped
10 ml (2 tsp) curry powder
2.5 ml (½ tsp) turmeric

Add the finely chopped ingredients, plus the spices. Mix well and let the mixture cook for 5 minutes.

1 small bay leaf
1 sprig thyme
a few parsley stalks
1 medium tomato, roughly chopped
200 ml (7 fl oz) fish stock (see page 195)

Add the herbs and tomato, then the fish stock. Bring to the boil, cover and allow to cook until the fish stock is reduced by half – about 15 minutes.

200 ml (7 fl oz) plain yoghurt or whipping cream
salt and freshly ground pepper

Stir in, and allow to cook together for 5–7 minutes. Season to taste.
Push everything through a sieve, or liquidise and sieve, and serve warm with the kedgeree.

TIP
You could, of course, make this curry sauce a little spicier, but as it's for breakfast, we don't really want it too strong.

GRILLED KIPPERS

Kippers are the most common smoked herring, and they should be plump, juicy and properly smoked – the best come from Loch Fyne and the Isle of Man. They should be golden rather than mahogany brown.

Scissor off the heads and lay, skin up, on foil in the grill pan. Grill until the skin begins to curl, about 2–3 minutes, then turn over, add a tiny knob of butter, and grill the other side for the same length of time. Serve with some lemon to squeeze over them and a garnish of watercress.

Kippers can also be 'jugged', another traditional way of preparing them. Put into a tall jug, pour boiling water over them, and leave for 10 minutes. Drain and serve with a knob of butter and some freshly ground black pepper. This keeps them very moist.

HERRING FILLETS IN OATMEAL

Herrings are a rich source of vitamins A and D, and many essential oils which are thought to prevent heart disease. Coating them in oatmeal is, not unexpectedly, a traditional way of preparing them in Scotland. (Trout is also cooked this way.) Once again, I've added a little extra. The herrings must be really fresh.

Serves 4

8 herring fillets	Check very carefully for any remaining bones.
120 ml (8 tbsp) fine oatmeal **1** apple, very finely grated salt and freshly ground pepper	Sprinkle on a plate, and mix well. Press the fillets into the apple meal to coat both sides.
30 ml (2 tbsp) vegetable oil for frying	Heat in a large frying pan and add the fillets. Fry for a few minutes on each side.
2 lemons, cut in half	Drain the fish well on kitchen paper, and serve each fillet with a half lemon to squeeze over.

TIP
Once you grate the apple, do work very quickly and fry as soon as you can. Otherwise the apple discolours.

GRILLED MARINATED KIPPERS

This is a more elaborate way of grilling kippers, but they are very moist and flavourful.

Serves 4

4 kipper fillets milk	The day before you wish to serve, soak fillets in enough milk to cover for 3 hours, then drain and dry.
60 ml (4 tbsp) olive oil freshly ground pepper **15 ml** (1 tbsp) chopped parsley **1** onion, finely chopped	Make a marinade by mixing all the ingredients. Marinate the kippers in a cool place overnight, or at least 3 hours, in a shallow dish, turning them once or twice.

200 g (7 oz) fresh white
  breadcrumbs, partially
  dried
	Remove the kippers, pat dry, and immediately roll them gently in the breadcrumbs.
	Grill at a high heat for 5 minutes on each side.

4 slices buttered brown bread	Serve with brown bread.

TIP

1 To knead a bread dough, place the ball of dough on a lightly floured board or work surface.

2 Fold the dough towards you, then push down and away, using the heels of your hands.

3 Fold again, give the dough a quarter turn, and repeat the process, developing a rocking action. (Kneading can also be done in a large mixer, using the dough hook and the slowest speed.)

SPICY QUARK BREAD

An interesting bread which is also very tasty at other times of day – with soup or cheese at lunch, for instance.

Serves 10

Oven: hot, 220°C/425°F/Gas 7

675 g (1½ lb) wholemeal flour, plus extra for sprinkling

Place in a bowl and make a well in the centre.

40 g (1½ oz) fresh yeast
or
20 g (¾ oz) dried yeast
a pinch of sugar
500 ml (18 fl oz) lukewarm water
oil for greasing

Dissolve the yeast and sugar in 450 ml (16 fl oz) of the lukewarm water, and pour into the well in the flour. Work to a thick dough in a mixer, using the dough hook.
Place in a lightly greased bowl, sprinkle with extra flour, cover the bowl with clingfilm and leave in a warm place to rise for approximately 15 minutes.

15 ml (1 tbsp) sea salt
15 ml (1 tbsp) coriander seeds
or
7.5 ml (½ tbsp) cumin seeds
2.5 ml (½ tsp) aniseed
2.5 ml (½ tsp) fennel seeds
250 g (9 oz) quark or fromage blanc (see page 200)

Dissolve the sea salt in the remaining lukewarm water, and add to the risen dough along with the seeds and the fromage blanc. Mix everything together well and knead for about 10 minutes.
Replace in the greased bowl, cover with clingfilm again, and allow to rise in the same warm place for about 45 minutes.
Knead the dough again and place in the bottom of a floured, slightly warmed bread basket with the fold facing upwards. Cover with a cloth and allow to rise in the warm place for a final 15 minutes. Put a dish holding about 100 ml (4 fl oz) hot water on the base of the oven and close the door.
Turn dough out on to a floured baking tray. Make slight crosswise incisions or prick with a fork all around the dough.
Put the tray on the bottom shelf of the preheated oven. Bake for 20 minutes, then reduce the temperature to 190°C/375°F/Gas 5 and bake for a further hour. Leave for 20 minutes with the oven turned off.
Allow to cool on a rack and leave for a few hours before cutting.

TIP
To make the coriander or cumin seeds more aromatic, roast in the oven for 6–8 minutes only. Crush the coriander lightly first.

M

APPLE MILLET CAKE

This light cake mixture can also be baked in patty tins for spicy muffins. Bake for twenty minutes only.

Makes a 25 cm (10 inch) cake

Oven: moderate, 180°C/350°F/Gas 4

4 egg yolks 70 g (2¾ oz) honey 5 ml (1 level tsp) powdered cinnamon 1 lemon, zested	Whisk together in a bowl until pale.
250 g (9 oz) apples, washed, cored and grated 80 g (3¼ oz) hazelnuts, chopped 30 ml (2 tbsp) raisins, chopped	Fold into the egg yolk mixture, one after the other.
80 g (3¼ oz) millet, finely ground 50 g (2 oz) wholemeal flour 5 ml (1 level tsp) baking powder	Mix together, then stir into the egg yolk mixture. Grease the cake tin, and sprinkle lightly with extra flour.
4 egg whites	Whisk until very stiff and fold into the mixture. Put into the tin, smooth down, and place on the bottom shelf of the oven. Bake for about an hour. Allow to stand for a further 10 minutes with the oven turned off. Cool on a wire rack in the tin, then carefully remove.

WALNUT AND RAISIN BREAD

This bread is delicious at any time of the day. It's good for breakfast and for lunch, but it makes the ideal accompaniment for prime cheeses at a special dinner party.

Makes 1 loaf

Oven: hot, 220°C/425°F/Gas 7

a little vegetable oil	Brush over a 450 g (1 lb) loaf tin.
150 g (5 oz) strong white flour, plus extra for dusting 150 g (5 oz) wheatmeal or wholewheat flour a good pinch of salt	Mix together in a bowl.

5 ml (1 tsp) butter	Rub in, and make a well in the centre.
10 g (⅓ oz) fresh yeast *or* **5 g** (⅙ oz) dried yeast **5 g** (⅙ oz) caster sugar **175 ml** (6 fl oz) lukewarm water	Dissolve the yeast and sugar in the water, then pour into the well. Mix to a dough. Knead on a lightly floured surface until soft and pliable. Adjust with extra flour if necessary. Place dough in the bottom of a large oiled bowl, cover with clingfilm, and leave for 40 minutes in a warm, draught-free place to rise. Squeeze the air from the dough, then return to the bowl for a further 20 minutes, covered. Form dough into a ball again. Cover and leave for 10 minutes in the same warm, draught-free place. Dust the table lightly with flour, then roll out dough very thinly to about 7 cm (2¾ in) thick.
100 g (4 oz) raisins **100 g** (4 oz) broken walnuts	Scatter evenly over the dough, then roll up like a Swiss roll and knead well to distribute the fruit and nuts evenly throughout the dough. Press into the oiled tin, and place in the same warm, draught-free place for 30 minutes to rise. Bake in the preheated oven for 35 minutes. Remove from the tin immediately, and cool on a wire rack for an hour at least.

ZOPF

This is a traditional bread from Switzerland which, like many milk breads, is plaited. Milk bread is by nature close-textured, but with a soft, tender crumb. It bakes to a marvellous, golden-brown sheen on the crust.

Makes 1 loaf	**Oven:** moderately hot, 190°C/375°F/Gas 5
750 g (1 lb 10 oz) unbleached white bread flour	Sift into a bowl and make a well in the centre.
350 ml (12 fl oz) lukewarm milk **30 g** (1¼ oz) fresh yeast *or* **15 g** (½ oz) dried yeast	Dissolve the yeast in the milk, whisking well. Pour into the well in the flour and mix together thoroughly. Knead well for a few minutes.
15 g (½ oz) salt **1 egg**, whisked **100 g** (4 oz) butter, softened	Mix together. Add to the bread dough and continue kneading until the dough becomes smooth and silky.
a little vegetable oil	Brush the bowl with oil, and place the dough in it. Leave for about 1½ hours in a warm, draught-free place, covered with clingfilm.

Squeeze the air from the dough by pressing with the palms. Knead again and leave for 15 minutes covered with the clingfilm (or under an upturned bowl).

Cut into three equal portions (use a scale to help). Roll these into long torpedo-shaped strands of equal lengths. Wait for a few minutes before continuing.

On a baking tray lined with silicone paper, lay the strands next to one another and, beginning in the centre, plait the pieces evenly towards you. Pinch the ends together firmly. Turn the tray and roll the plait over. Complete plaiting the other side, and pinch the ends. Turn ends underneath.

1 egg 5 ml (1 tsp) salt	Whisk together to form a glaze, then brush generously over the plaited loaf. Leave to rise again in a warm place until doubled in bulk. Glaze again with gentleness and care, and bake for 30–35 minutes in the preheated oven. Leave to cool on a cooling rack. Do not slice until cold.

WHOLEMEAL CROISSANTS

These are delicious – and healthy – served for a special, probably weekend, breakfast. Allow at least 7 hours for making the dough.

Makes 18

Oven: hot, 220°C/425°F/Gas 7

30 g (1¼ oz) caster sugar 10 ml (2 tsp) salt 300 ml (½ pint) lukewarm water	Dissolve sugar and salt in one-third of the water in a jug.
20 g (¾ oz) fresh yeast *or* 10 g (a good ¼ oz) dried yeast 25 g (1 oz) dried milk powder (or 1 egg)	In a separate bowl, whisk into the remaining water.
250 g (9 oz) strong plain bread flour 250 g (9 oz) wheatmeal flour	Place in a bowl (or in an electric mixer) and mix in first the sugar and salt liquid, then the yeast mixture. Beat until well blended and the dough comes away from the sides of the bowl. Do not overwork.
a little oil	Put dough in the base of a large oiled bowl and cover with clingfilm. Leave to rise in a warm place for about 30–45 minutes. It should double in size. Squeeze the air out of the dough with your hands, and knead a little. Cut a cross in the top of the dough.

flour for dusting	On a lightly floured surface, roll out the ball of dough in four places, making a quarter turn each time so that there are four 'petals' around a central piece.
300 g (11 oz) butter, firm, but not too hard	Flatten out butter to a tile shape, with square edges. Place in the centre of the dough, and fold the four 'petals' over it, completely enclosing the butter. Roll the dough away from you carefully into a rectangle about 40 × 70 cm (16 × 28 in). Fold dough into three, wrap in oiled polythene and chill for at least 45 minutes. Repeat this rolling, folding and chilling process twice more, rolling with the fold on the left each time. The work surface should be lightly dusted with flour each time as well. Roll the dough out to a 45 cm (18 in) square. Trim the edges then cut into nine 15 cm (6 in) squares. Cut these squares in half diagonally to make eighteen triangles. (You could use a butter paper folded into a triangle as a template if you liked.) Arrange the triangles on baking sheets, cover tightly with polythene and chill for a few minutes. Place the triangles, one at a time, on the work surface with the point away from you. Starting at the base, roll up each triangle loosely with the point underneath. Squeeze the ends gently and curve the rolls into a crescent shape, and space out on the baking sheets, pointed end beneath. Cover loosely and leave to rise in a very warm, draught-free place until doubled in size, about 1–2 hours.
1 egg yolk, beaten with 15 ml (1 tbsp) milk	Brush very lightly over each croissant, then bake in the preheated oven for 15 minutes. Transfer to a cooling rack immediately.

TIP
You don't have to get up at the crack of dawn to make these croissants for breakfast. You can make the dough and bake the croissants for 10 minutes the day before, then put in freezer while still a little warm. The next morning, bake for about 10 minutes.

Cutting and shaping croissants.

BLUEBERRY MUFFINS

Delicious little mouthfuls which could be the finale of a magnificently healthy breakfast.

Makes 20–24	**Oven:** moderately hot, 200°C/400°F/Gas 6
50 g (2 oz) butter, melted	Use about 10 ml (2 tsp) to grease muffin cups or patty tins.
250 g (9 oz) plain white flour **25 g** (1 oz) baking powder **5 ml** (1 tsp) salt **60 g** (2¼ oz) caster sugar	Sift together into a bowl, then blend in the remaining melted butter.
2 eggs, beaten **200 ml** (7 fl oz) milk ½ lemon, zested a drop of vanilla extract	Mix in.
100 g (4 oz) blueberries	Fold in, then fill the muffin cups or patty tins. Bake in the preheated oven for approximately 20 minutes.
icing sugar to dust	Sprinkle with a little icing sugar to decorate.

TIP

Other fruits could be used instead of blueberries – blackberries and cranberries, for instance – or they could be made plain (one-third of the flour could also be wholewheat).

The muffins freeze well, and could be batch-baked, frozen, then defrosted overnight and warmed through in the oven for breakfast.

DRIED FRUIT CONSERVE

Dried fruits such as apricots and prunes make very good conserves – and they're so simple. All you need do is cook your fruit in as little water as possible until soft, and then liquidise it into a thick purée. In the normal way, you would add plenty of sugar and boil as for a traditional jam, but in this fashion the flavour of the fruit is perfectly retained. The conserve must, however, be kept in the refrigerator, and used within a week. Fresh fruits could be prepared in this way too.

Fruit conserves can be used as fillings for pies, tartlets, pancakes, on hot toast or scones, on top of muesli, or mixed into some freshly made yoghurt.

Makes about 500 g (18 oz)

450 g (1 lb) dried apricots (or prunes)	Wash and soak overnight in water. The next day, discard the water, and transfer the fruit to a shallow saucepan.
apple (or lemon) juice	Pour over enough to just cover: you want finally to have a very thick purée. Simmer very gently, uncovered, for about 30 minutes or until thoroughly cooked and soft. (Remove prune stones.) Cool and then process, liquidise or sieve to a thick, smooth consistency.
5 ml (1 tsp) finely zested orange (or lemon) peel	Add, stir, and store in the refrigerator.

TIP
The conserve should be stored in very clean, small glass jars which have been rinsed in boiling water. It could also be stored in appropriate clean containers in the freezer – which is what we do in Switzerland.

THREE-FRUIT MARMALADE

Marmalade seems uniquely British to me (it's Scottish actually), although it is traditionally made with the Seville oranges that come from much sunnier climes. Apparently it all started when a Mrs Keiller of Dundee used up some of the new fruit her husband had bought from a ship in the port in a preserve she usually made with quinces (or *marmelo* in Portuguese). The name marmalade is now applied to citrus fruit preserves, and this one has a fine flavour.

Makes about 2.25 kg (5 lb)

675 g (1½ lb) mixed citrus fruit (roughly 225 g/8 oz each of grapefruit, oranges and lemons)	Wash and dry well. Cut each into quarters and then slice thinly, carefully retaining juice and pips.
1.5 litres (2½ pints) water	Tie the pips in a muslin bag, and put the slices and juice into a preserving pan with the water. Tie the muslin bag to the handle of the pan so that it is well suspended in the liquid. Bring the contents of the pan to the boil, and cook gently for about 2 hours. Lift out the bag of pips and squeeze it between two spoons to get out the all-important pectin.
1.25 kg (2¾ lb) preserving sugar	Add, and heat gently, stirring, until dissolved. Bring to the boil and boil rapidly until setting point is reached – about 15–20 minutes. Test (see below), and if not ready, continue boiling and test again. Remove scum from surface, cool for about 5–10 minutes then stir to distribute the peel before potting in warm sterilised jars. Seal well while still hot with wax discs and then cellophane covers or lids. Label and store in a dry, cool and dark place. Will keep for about 1 year.

TIP
The easiest way to test for setting is with a thermometer: warm this first then insert when the pan is off the heat – it should read 104°C (220°F). If you haven't got a thermometer, put a plate in the freezer to cool. Put 5 ml (1 tsp) marmalade on the plate and allow to cool. Push the surface with a finger, and if it wrinkles, it's ready.

STRAWBERRY ORANGE JUICE

Freshly squeezed orange juice is a marvellous way to start the day: it's fresh, enlivening, and rich in vitamin C. You could mix in a few cut strawberries for a nice (and very simple) summer variation. Some champagne would be delicious too . . .

Makes about 1.2 litres (just over 2 pints)

75–100 g (3–4 oz) fresh strawberries, hulled and sliced

1.1 litres (2 pints) fresh orange juice (about 12 oranges)

Purée in a blender until smooth.
Strain if desired, then chill. Drink within a few hours of making, the sooner the better.

BREAKFAST COCKTAIL

I like this instead of breakfast if I'm in a hurry, and often serve it in tall glasses at brunch. It's soothing, filling and delicious, and particularly welcome after exercise – a run or a game of squash. Adjust the proportions of the ingredients to taste.

Serves 4

600 ml (1 pint) skimmed milk

175 ml (6 fl oz) fresh orange juice

30 ml (2 tbsp) plain yoghurt

1–2 ripe bananas, peeled and chopped

1 ripe mango, peeled and stoned

Place all the ingredients in the blender, and whizz up until frothy.
Pour into glasses.

freshly grated nutmeg

Dust lightly with a little nutmeg if you like.

FRUIT TEAS

Tea was introduced to Great Britain in the middle of the seventeenth century, and it has become inextricably associated with the British ever since. I like tea very much, and I think it is a very good breakfast drink (better than coffee, which contains too much caffeine). I don't serve it plain, though, as I like to experiment and pep up Earl Grey or Darjeeling teas with other flavours.

These other flavours come from fruit or fruit peelings which I dry. It's a very simple process. Stretch muslin over a wire cake tray and fasten tightly with safety pins or staples. Set your oven as low as it can go – usually 110°C/225°F/Gas ¼. Place your prepared fruit or peelings on the muslin tray and simply put in the oven for several hours.

Pieces of peel – of apple, mango, citrus fruit – will take about 2 hours. Whole raspberries will take about 3 hours. (Many other whole, halved or sliced fruits can be dried in this way, for use *as* dried fruits. Experiment. Herbs are dried similarly as well, but for a very much shorter time.)

When the peelings are leathery, cool thoroughly, and store carefully in a dry place. Or you can chop them immediately into small pieces and add to a packet or tin of leaf tea, to which they will gradually add their aroma. When the tea is made in the normal way – boiling water added to the leaves – the peelings will give out flavour as well.

You can make mixed teas too – I like the combination of raspberry and apple particularly, and I always garnish a cup with a sprig of fresh mint.

SPICED TEA

Assam or Darjeeling teas could be used – the former makes the revitalising, ruddy tea which traditionally stood all day on the hob without becoming bitter (Yorkshire and Ireland). Ceylon tea is milder, more refreshing, not quite so strong, and is ideal for this spiced tea.

Makes about 850 ml (1½ pints)

2 strips lemon zest
2 cloves
4 cm (1½ inch) cinnamon
    stick
3 allspice berries
950 ml (a scant 1¾ pints)
    water

Bring to the boil and then simmer for 6 minutes. Bring back to the boil.

90 g (3½ oz) Indian or Ceylon tea leaves	Strain immediately over the tea leaves in a warmed teapot. Leave to infuse for about 5 minutes in the usual way.
lemon slices, finely cut	Strain into cups, and float a lemon slice in each.
honey	Add to taste.

SUNDAY LUNCH

Sunday is a traditional day of rest in most Christian countries, and for many people all over Europe, not just in Britain, it is a time when families and friends meet to enjoy a relaxing meal together. In this country, this meal usually has a roast meat as its centrepiece – the 'roast beef of olde England' being the most famous – with a vegetable soup to begin, and a fruit pudding to follow.

Britain should be proud of her basic ingredients. The beef, particularly Aberdeen Angus, is second to none, and the lambs grazed on the lush grasses of the South Downs, of Wales and on the hillsides of the Dales are amongst the most flavourful I have ever tasted. The fruit and vegetables grown in this country are superb as well, and there is a host of old and famous recipes which make full and good use of them. I find it sad that so many chefs tend to import food from Europe; with the exception of one or two items, there's really no reason at all to go elsewhere.

Many of these traditional dishes, however, are not as healthy as we might wish in these days of increasing knowledge about the ill-effects of animal fats and cholesterol, of over-eating, and lack of exercise. So here I have explored many of the recipes so well known to Sunday lunchers, and have shown, I hope, how they might be improved as far as health is concerned. In my book *Cuisine Naturelle*, I discussed how foods can be cooked, eaten – and enjoyed – without oil, butter, cream, alcohol, and with as little sugar and salt as possible. Healthier alternatives were substituted – such as natural yoghurt and fromage blanc for instance – and cooking techniques adapted. Steaming, braising, poaching, grilling and dry sautéing are all basic methods of preparation which don't need added fat, and all of them allow the natural flavours of the food to come through – to me, one of the most vital elements in cooking.

Although many of the recipes following do not adhere to the purest principles of Cuisine Naturelle – a truly traditional Yorkshire pudding, for instance, would never pass muster! – I have hinted at ways in which they might turn in a healthier direction.

Stock and Soups

A good stock is the first necessity for a good soup or sauce, and you will find many of my basic recipes on pages 192–6. The more flavourful stocks are, the better the eventual soup or sauce will taste. They're easy to make, too, simmering gently away on the stove while you get on with other things. They can be reduced to intensify flavours, vital for the best gravies and sauces. Stocks can be stored in the freezer, where they are always available for virtually immediate use.

There is a tradition of creamy vegetable soups in this country, and many of them are quite delicious – and not too rich if the fat and cream content is reduced. However, with a good tasty stock such as the vegetable one on page 192, you could serve a vegetable consommé with a garnish of fresh leaves and herbs, and it will contain no calories whatsoever. A light soup such as this might actually be the best dish to serve before a roast meat main course, as it will not detract from those delights to come.

The Main Course

Roast beef remains the epitome of the British Sunday, but red meat is less popular now than it used to be, for both health and cost reasons. Indeed, because of beef prices, many people can only afford to buy and cook it infrequently – which makes it an occasional treat, an indulgence which cannot do anyone any harm. Beef was once cooked on a spit over a fire, basting itself with fat as it turned, and the fat dripping away. Roasting in modern ovens often means the meat sits in its fat, but I have suggested ways in which this may be avoided. My Cuisine Naturelle version of a beef joint uses no fat at all. The roast potatoes, too, cook in the meat juices instead of the fat; a Cuisine Naturelle alternative would be a baked potato with a flavourful garnish of virtually fat-free fromage frais instead of soured cream or butter. Even my gravy method may be better for you, as it does away with the need for flour as thickening.

There seemed no possible way of changing something so quintessentially British as Yorkshire pudding – but the herb addition could not be criticised by even the most conservative Yorkshireman as it tastes so good! Horseradish is another traditional accompaniment to beef, good just freshly grated on to the meat itself, rather than mixed with cream.

Other traditional Sunday lunch main courses are stews or braises, and the best of these, I think, are Lancashire hotpot and braised oxtail. I scoured my collection of old cookery books to try and find the ultimate recipe, but all the sources differed – so eventually I concocted my own version. Both dishes are typically English, using good basic ingredients, being cooked in a simple way, and are very comforting and satisfying.

Vegetables almost always seem to be overcooked, which is such a shame, as most only need moments of cooking. I like mine really crunchy There are a few ideas here, particularly for cabbage, the cliché *bête-noire* of British vegetable cuisine.

Desserts

England became known as the nation of 'pudding eaters' after the fashion for heavy and rich desserts, encouraged by the enthusiastic pudding-eating monarch, George I. Many of these don't appeal, but a bread and butter pudding made *my* way, that is something quite different! Fruit pies have been popular for centuries, but by using featherlight sheets of filo pastry instead of shortcrust (filo is the only pastry used in Cuisine Naturelle), the fat and starch content of any dish is cut immediately. Poached or baked fruits are very much healthier, and should always be served with an alternative to cream such as natural yoghurt.

I hope that my interpretations of some British dishes will make for an enlightened and heightened enjoyment of many Sunday lunches to come.

VEGETABLE SOUP

Make this soup with the freshly made vegetable stock (see page 192), and its aromatic vegetables. A good way to start lunch on a cold day. You can reduce the cream content if you wish.

Serves 10

275 g (10 oz) potatoes, peeled salt	Cut about three-quarters of the potatoes into even sizes and cook in lightly salted water until soft. Cut the remaining potatoes into dice and cook separately as above until just done. Drain and keep warm.
cooked vegetables from the stock preparation	Purée with the potato pieces and then press through a sieve.
1.5 litres (2½ pints) vegetable stock	Stir into the puréed vegetables and heat in a pan.
300 ml (½ pint) single cream freshly ground pepper	Add, reheat, but do not boil, and adjust seasoning. Serve in individual soup bowls, garnished with the warmed potato dice.
a few sprigs of marjoram	Add a few leaves to each serving.

PEA SOUP

Pea soup is a particularly British dish, which often uses ham stock, as the flavours of peas and bacon or ham go so well together. The combination dates from the Middle Ages (and not just in Britain), when bacon and dried peas were part of the staple winter diet. (The fogs that once afflicted London were called 'pea soupers' after one such thick soup!) This lighter version is very briefly cooked, and frozen peas can be used when fresh are not in season. The soup could also be served cold.

Serves 4

1 medium onion, chopped **2** rashers back bacon, rinded **25 g** (1 oz) butter	Lightly sweat onion and bacon in the butter.
300 g (11 oz) peas, shelled	Add and allow to cook for a few minutes.
500 ml (18 fl oz) vegetable or light chicken stock (see pages 192 and 193)	Add, and bring to the boil. Skim and simmer gently for about 5 minutes. Remove the bacon and cut into small pieces. Set aside. Purée the soup in a blender then pass through a sieve. Bring back to the boil.
50 ml (2 fl oz) whipping cream	Whip cream then whisk into the soup to make it light and frothy.
salt and freshly ground pepper	Taste for seasoning.
¼ lettuce, finely shredded **2** slices medium-sliced bread, cut into 6 mm (¼ in) cubes and fried in clarified butter	Use, with the diced bacon, to garnish the soup.

TIP
To clarify butter, heat 100 g (4 oz) butter gently in a pan until there is foam on the top. Simmer for another 3–5 minutes – do not allow to brown – then skim well and pour off into a bowl, ideally through muslin. Any solids still left will sink to the bottom of the bowl to be scraped off the solid clarified butter when set. There will be about 50–75 g (2–3 oz) butter.

CHILLED TOMATO AND ORANGE SOUP

A refreshing soup for a summer Sunday lunch.

Serves 6

90 g (3½ oz) carrot **60 g** (2½ oz) onion **30 g** (1¼ oz) leek ½ clove garlic, crushed **20 g** (¾ oz) butter	Coarsely chop vegetables, and place with the garlic and butter in a suitable pan. Soften and colour lightly.
400 g (14 oz) tomatoes **1** bouquet garni (see below) **500 ml** (18 fl oz) vegetable stock (see page 192)	Add, bring to the boil, and skim. Simmer until the vegetables are cooked, about 20 minutes. Remove the bouquet garni.
a pinch of sugar	Add, then put vegetables and stock through a sieve. Cool.
50 ml (2 fl oz) double cream **2** oranges, juiced	Stir in, then chill.
salt and freshly ground pepper	Taste for seasoning.
2 oranges, segmented (see page 6)	Garnish each bowl with two segments.

TIP

It's very easy to make a bouquet garni at home. Place a piece of muslin on the work surface and put on it some parsley stalks, 1 bay leaf, some peppercorns, a sprig of thyme, a little celeriac and carrot. Wrap up and tie. You could also wrap and tie in a leek leaf. Bouquet garnis are infinitely variable in content, depending on flavourings available or in season, and on the recipe.

VEGETABLE BOUILLON WITH SPINACH

Nothing could be simpler – or healthier – than this clear bouillon garnished with fresh young spinach leaves. I often add some mushrooms and tomatoes to the vegetables for the stock to give extra flavour to the bouillon.

Serves 10

1.5 litres (2½ pints) vegetable stock (see page 192)	Pour into a clean pan.
about **225 g** (8 oz) very small young leaves of spinach	Wash very carefully, and spin or pat dry. Divide among the soup plates.
salt and freshly ground pepper	Heat the stock to boiling, season to taste, then ladle into the plates.
1 small bunch of fresh chervil	Garnish each with the chervil leaves.

CUCUMBER AND YOGHURT SOUP

A nourishing and light soup to start a Sunday lunch to be eaten in the garden perhaps.

Serves 4

½ cucumber, peeled, cut in half and seeded salt	Grate cucumber coarsely, cutting a few matchstick batons for a garnish. Sprinkle with salt and leave in a colander for 30 minutes. Rinse and drain.
400 g (14 oz) low-fat plain yoghurt ½ clove garlic, crushed **5 ml** (1 tsp) white wine vinegar **15 ml** (1 tbsp) cut dill **10 ml** (2 tsp) chopped mint	Mix together with the grated cucumber in a bowl. If it becomes too thick, work in a few tablespoons of water.
salt and freshly ground white pepper	Cover the bowl and place in the refrigerator for 2 hours. Season to taste with salt and pepper.
a few sprigs of dill	Just before serving, garnish with dill and the cucumber batons.

Cucumber and Yoghurt Soup
(opposite)

ROAST RIBS OF BEEF

Meat cooked on the bone is quite delicious (as are fish and chicken), because most of the flavour is near the bone. Season meat before cooking, despite the fact that salt can draw moisture out; once the meat is cooked, the pores are closed and seasoning then will have no effect.

Serves 10

Oven: very hot, 240°C/475°F/Gas 9

1 forerib of beef, about 5 ribs, trimmed and tied
20 tiny sprigs herbs (rosemary or thyme)
sea salt and freshly ground pepper

Push as many herb sprigs as you can between the flesh and the layer of fat on the beef. Season well all over.

a little dripping

Heat in a roasting tin on top of the stove.

1.8 kg (4 lb) extra beef bones (if available)

Add with the joint of beef. Brown the bones and joint all over. Place the joint on top of the bones.
Place in the preheated oven and roast for 20 minutes. Turn the oven temperature down to 200°C/400°F/Gas 6, and cook for a further 1½ hours, basting every now and again.
About 30–40 minutes after first putting the meat in the oven, remove the bones and dripping from the pan. Return joint to oven to continue cooking. (Keep the bones for the gravy.)
About 25 minutes before meat is cooked, skim off the fat from the meat juices in the tin (and add the potatoes). Return to the oven and continue cooking.
Remove the beef from the roasting tin and rest in a warm place for about 20–25 minutes before carving.

TIP
Good quality young beef should be red and have white fat. The older the animal gets, the more yellow the fat becomes. Ask the butcher to trim and tie the joint for you.

BEEF RIB WITH HERBS

This is the Cuisine Naturelle version of 'roast beef', which uses no extra fat at all in the cooking. It is important that the butcher prepares this well. He must cut the meat absolutely flat and level with the bone or it will not cook evenly. Use a heavy iron ridged frying pan, or a grill pan designed for use on the stove. You could also grill the meat with heat from *above*.

Serves 2

1 wing rib of beef, approx 550 g (1¼ lb)	Trim well, and check that it will fit in the pan.
30 ml (2 tbsp) mixed herbs (sage, rosemary and thyme), finely chopped **1** clove garlic, crushed	Rub the flesh with the herbs and garlic. Leave to marinate for 2–3 hours. To grill, heat up the pan. Remove the herbs from the beef, chop and retain.
salt and freshly ground pepper	Season the meat, place in the pan and grill for 4–5 minutes before turning over. Pour off any fat that collects in the pan. Grill the other side for another 4–5 minutes, according to how you like it cooked. Sprinkle the herbs over the meat just before it's cooked. Remove and keep in a warm place to rest for 8–10 minutes before carving diagonally into neat slices.

TIP
Salt is a mineral required by the body in small amounts, but in excess can contribute to high blood pressure and strokes. By using herbs and herb mixtures (see page 197), the amount of salt needed in cooking can be considerably reduced (although the flavours of the herbs must never overpower the dish in which they are used).

YORKSHIRE PUDDING

Use a small roasting pan, about 25 cm (10 in) in diameter. Once Yorkshire pudding was cooked under spit-roast meat, taking advantage of the dripping that would otherwise have been wasted. The herbs aren't in the least traditional, but they taste good.

Serves 12	**Oven:** moderately hot, 200°C/400°F/Gas 6
dripping from the beef	Pass through a fine conical sieve, and lightly coat the base and sides of the pudding tin. Put in the top of the oven to heat.
350 g (12 oz) plain flour salt and freshly ground pepper	Sift into a bowl, and make a well in the centre. Season to taste.
5 medium eggs, lightly whisked **600 ml** (1 pint) milk **300 ml** (½ pint) water	Mix the eggs with a little of the mixed milk and water. Pour into the well in the flour and, with a wooden spoon, stir from the middle, gradually incorporating the flour. Beat well to get rid of any lumps, to a creamy consistency. Add the remainder of the liquid, and mix well together.
30 ml (2 tbsp) chopped mixed herbs (sage, thyme, parsley, etc)	Mix in when the batter is smooth. Pour into the smoking hot tin, replace in the top of the oven, and cook for 30 minutes, alongside the meat. When you remove the beef, reduce the temperature to 180°C/350°F/Gas 4 and continue cooking the pudding for another 20 minutes (a total of about 50 minutes). Serve, cut in squares, with the beef.

TIP

Sieves come in all sizes and materials, and should be chosen according to your needs: never use metal other than stainless steel, for instance, when sieving some fruits or vinegars. A tamis or wooden drum sieve, although large, is useful for seedless fruit purées, for dry ingredients and smooth sauces. A stainless steel chinois, or conical sieve (named because of its shape, rather like a Chinese coolie's hat) is useful, and comes in fine or coarser mesh. The former is so fine it can duplicate the function of muslin for straining consommé or jelly. A handle clips over the side of a pan, the food is inserted, and the solids are trapped in the tip of the cone, the liquid draining through the sides. A rotary ricer with stand is similar to the chinois, but comes with a tapered pestle to work foods through the cone.

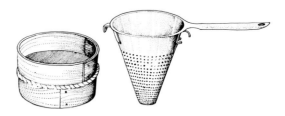

A GOOD GRAVY

Befriend your butcher and always ask for extra bones cut into pieces when buying a joint for roasting: it won't cost either of you very much. The flavour of meat on the bones is good, and using them partially roasted makes for a stronger and more delicious gravy. All the vegetables and herbs together should not weigh more than 6 oz (175 g), or they may overpower the rich, meaty flavour.

Serves 10

1.8 kg (4 lb) roasted beef bones, cut small	Place in a large, shallow saucepan.
1 medium carrot **1** medium onion, halved and charred on a hot plate or pan **1** stick celery ½ leek, washed	Chop all the vegetables and add them to the pan. Sweat for about 5–6 minutes in the dry pan, to colour slightly.
1 sprig each of rosemary and thyme **1** bay leaf	Tie the herbs together and add.
2.5 litres (4 pints) water (or beef or vegetable stock)	Add 300 ml (½ pint) of the water (or stock) and simmer briskly until the liquid has reduced to almost nothing. Add about the same amount of water (or stock), and simmer once more to reduce. This reduction each time concentrates the flavours beautifully. Just barely cover the bones and vegetables with the remaining liquid, and bring to the boil. Reduce the heat, skim to remove fat and froth, then simmer for about an hour until it has a good flavour. Pass through a fine sieve or cloth into another pan. Bring back to the boil, check the seasoning, and reduce further as desired. Allow to stand for 15 minutes then remove all surface fat with paper towels.

ROAST POTATOES

Serves 10	Oven: moderately hot, 200°C/400°F/Gas 6
1.4–1.8 kg (3–4 lb) tiny new potatoes	Scrub well, but do not peel. Dry thoroughly. When you remove the dripping finally from the beef, put the potatoes in the same pan. Turn them around in the meat juices so that they are well coated. Return to the oven and cook for the remainder of the beef cooking time, a further 20 minutes.
salt and freshly ground pepper	Season and keep warm with the meat while you finish the Yorkshire pudding.

BAKED POTATOES

Choose potatoes about the size of a large egg, aiming to serve two per person. With no fat used in the cooking, this is a healthy alternative to conventional roast potatoes.

Serves 10	Oven: moderately hot, 190–200°C/375–400°F/Gas 5–6
about **1.8 kg** (4 lb) small to medium potatoes	Scrub the potatoes well, dry, then wrap individually in foil. Bake in the oven for about 30 minutes, or until tender.
100 g (4 oz) fromage frais **15 ml** (1 tbsp) finely cut chives lemon juice to taste sea salt and freshly ground pepper	Mix together and season to taste. Cut a cross in the surface of each potato and squeeze from below. Spoon over the fromage frais mixture.

STEAMED BABY CABBAGES

At last growers in this country are listening to their customers. The very young vegetables which are becoming increasingly available are bursting with flavour.

Per person	
approx **3** baby cabbages, washed salt and freshly ground pepper	Open out the leaves a little, so heat can penetrate to the centre. Place in a steamer, and season to taste.
25 g (1 oz) onion, finely sliced	Sweat briefly in a non-stick pan until it has softened a little. Place on top of the cabbages, cover, and steam for approximately 2–3 minutes, or until the hearts are just tender. Check seasoning and serve immediately.

BRAISED CABBAGE

Cabbage has a bad reputation, due entirely to the fact that it is always overcooked. Just braised or steamed so that it is still crisp, it is a delicious vegetable.

Serves 10

2 medium Savoy cabbages, chopped	Wash briefly, then dry very well.
4 rashers bacon, rind removed, finely cut 1 onion, peeled and finely sliced 20 ml (1 tbsp) vegetable oil	In a large shallow pan, sweat the bacon and onion in the oil.
25 g (1 oz) carrots, peeled, scored (see page 117) and sliced salt and freshly ground pepper	Add, with the cabbage. Season and moisten with a little water. Cover the pan. Cook for 5–6 minutes, then remove the lid. Give the cabbage a stir and check for seasoning. It should be just cooked.

BRAISED OXTAIL WITH GARDEN VEGETABLES

The full flavour of oxtail is released through long slow cooking. For a very relaxed Sunday, you could cook it the day before and leave to cool overnight when the fat will solidify on the top. Remove and reheat the stew. Any garden vegetables will do – you could use baby carrots, baby corn, cauliflower and courgettes as in the photograph.

Serves 4

Ingredients	Method
16 pieces oxtail, well trimmed salt and freshly ground pepper **20 g** (¾ oz) plain flour	Season the oxtail, and dust with the flour.
50 ml (2 fl oz) vegetable oil	Heat in a large frying pan, and brown the oxtail well. You'll probably need to do this in batches. Remove from the pan and set aside. Clean pan gently with kitchen paper.
20 g (¾ oz) butter **150 g** (5 oz) mixed onion, carrot and celery, very finely diced ½ garlic clove, finely chopped	Add to the pan, and sauté lightly.
100 ml (4 fl oz) red wine	Pour in and deglaze the pan. Transfer into a suitably large, heavy saucepan.
50 g (2 oz) diced tomato	Add along with the oxtail.
2.5 litres (4½ pints) brown beef stock (see page 194)	Add 500 ml (18 fl oz) to the pan, and reduce to a caramel. Repeat this once more, then add stock to cover the oxtail.
1 bay leaf **2** sprigs thyme	Add, and leave to simmer for 2½-3 hours, or until the meat is tender. Add more stock as necessary. Remove the oxtail from the sauce and discard the vegetables and herbs. Strain the sauce, bring to the boil, and skim until all grease is removed. Put the oxtail back into the sauce and place in a dish.
50 g (2 oz) each of carrot, swede and turnip, turned and blanched **50 g** (2 oz) button onions, peeled and blanched **25 g** (1 oz) small mangetout **25 g** (1 oz) butter	Heat the garnish vegetables through in a pan with the butter, season, and spoon over the oxtail.
15 g (½ oz) parsley, finely chopped	Sprinkle over the meat and vegetables, and serve.

M

47

LANCASHIRE HOTPOT

Traditionally, a tall pot is used, so that the chops can stand upright. Oysters were once added, and the dish got its name from the fact that it would be taken, wrapped in a blanket, to the races – kept this way, it would remain hot for quite a long time.

Serves 10

Oven: moderate, 160–180°C/325–350°F/Gas 3–4

10 lamb loin chops **10** middle neck lamb chops **10** lamb's kidneys	Trim the meats of fat, and halve, clean and core the kidneys.
800 g (1¾ lb) onions, sliced **50 ml** (2 fl oz) olive oil	Sweat and lightly colour the onion in the oil.
salt and freshly ground pepper	Season the meats with salt and pepper, then stand the loin chops, 'tails' up, on the bottom of a suitably large, tall pot.
800 g (1¾ lb) carrots, cut in pieces	Scatter some of the carrot and onion on top, filling any holes and spaces. Season again.
500 g (18 oz) button mushrooms, trimmed	Add with the kidneys, and some more carrot and onion. Press slightly so that the surface is flat. Season. Arrange the middle neck chops and cover with remaining carrot and onion. Season again.
1.5 kg (3¼ lb) medium potatoes, peeled and sliced	Arrange neatly, slightly overlapping, over the top of the ingredients. Brush with a little oil, and season.
850 ml (1½ pints) lamb stock (see page 194)	Pour in until it almost covers the potatoes.
a few sprigs of herbs to taste	Add. Cover with the lid and bake in the oven slowly for 1½–2 hours. Remove the lid for the last 30 minutes to allow the potatoes to become golden brown.

MIXED VEGETABLE GRATIN

The vegetables for this dish may be changed according to taste and availability – large runner beans would be good, for instance (cut into diamonds). It makes a tasty accompaniment vegetable dish, or an ideal hors d'oeuvre.

Serves 10

Oven: moderately hot, 200°C/400°F/Gas 6

600 ml (1 pint) vegetable stock (see page 192) **50 g** (2 oz) butter a pinch of salt	Bring half the stock to the boil with the butter and some salt.
500 g (18 oz) beans, cut into strips **250 g** (9 oz) carrots, scrubbed, trimmed and sliced **250 g** (9 oz) turnips, peeled and sliced	Put each vegetable separately into the boiling stock and blanch. Stop the cooking by plunging into the cold remaining stock (this retains the flavours). Drain the vegetables, and arrange in a gratin dish.
3 medium tomatoes, skinned and seeded	Cut into thin fillets, and add.
2 egg yolks, mixed with a fork **175 ml** (6 fl oz) whipping cream, whipped freshly ground pepper	Fold together, season to taste with salt and pepper, and pour over the vegetables.
50 g (2 oz) freshly grated Parmesan cheese	Sprinkle over the vegetables, and bake in the preheated oven for 10–12 minutes until lightly set.

TIP

Blanching generally means immersing a food in boiling water and boiling for a very short time before plunging into cold water or stock (or placing the whole pan in a bain-marie of ice) to stop the cooking. (Some foods, like meat, meat bones for stock, and chicken, are brought to the boil in *cold* liquid.) Blanching is usually preliminary to other methods of cooking, helping to retain vitamins and colour in green vegetables particularly; it is also necessary before freezing vegetables, as it inactivates enzymes and sets the colour. Blanching can also soften leaves for 'wrapping', for instance, and remove skins from vegetables and fruit such as tomatoes and peaches. Two large pans are necessary, one for the boiling, and one for the cold liquid. A blanching basket whereby the items can be inserted then lifted out quickly is very useful.

Left: Ratatouille en Pâte Filo (page 179). *Right:* Mixed Vegetable Gratin (opposite)

COURGETTES WITH TOMATOES

A simple braise, which could be adapted for other seasonal vegetables – try okra, for instance, instead of the courgettes.

Serves 10

3 medium onions, peeled and cut into small pieces	Place in a large non-stick pan, and sauté for about 4–5 minutes.
1.25 kg (2¾ lb) courgettes, washed, trimmed and cut into large dice	Add to the pan, and sauté for another 5 minutes.
1.25 kg (2¾ lb) tomatoes, seeded and chopped salt and freshly ground pepper about **15 ml** (1 tbsp) finely chopped fresh oregano	Spread over the vegetables and season. Cover the pan, place on the heat and sweat the vegetables for 2–3 minutes, shaking the pan occasionally. Transfer to a heated dish just before serving.
15–20 fresh basil leaves	Tear into small pieces and sprinkle over.

BAKED APPLES

It was apparently the Romans who introduced many of the fruit we now consider to be quintessentially British. Fruit, like vegetables, were thought to be best cooked, and apples baked in this way are very traditional.

Serves 10	**Oven:** moderately hot, 190°C/375°F/Gas 5
10 medium dessert apples, washed	Pare a 5 mm (¼ in) wide strip of skin around the middle of the apples, then core.
100 g (4 oz) unsalted butter	Use some of the butter to grease a flat buttered dish. Place the apples in the dish.
100 g (4 oz) dark brown sugar **100 g** (4 oz) raisins a pinch of powdered cinnamon	Mix together, and spoon into the apple centres. Top each apple with a flake of butter.
200–300 ml (7–10 fl oz) white wine	Add to the dish: it should be about 1.5 cm (¾ in) deep. Bake in the preheated oven for about 40 minutes until the apples are tender but still hold their shape.

PEARS POACHED IN RED WINE

Poached or stewed pears have long been enjoyed in Britain, and used to be served from market stalls at an annual fair in Devon, accompanied by that county's finest clotted cream.

Serves 4

4 Comice pears	Peel and core carefully, leaving the stems on.
400 ml (14 fl oz) red wine **50 ml** (2 fl oz) water **50 g** (2 oz) sugar **25 g** (1 oz) honey ½ cinnamon stick	In a pan large enough to hold the pears upright, heat together. Place the pears in the pan, stems up, and poach them at just below boiling point until soft, about 10–12 minutes. Remove the pears, and boil the wine to reduce to a syrupy consistency. Cool.
a few strips of lemon and orange zest, cut into matchsticks	Blanch for about 1 minute in boiling water. Drain and cool. When pears, syrup and citrus zest are cold, place the pears in a dish, and moisten with the syrup.
4 sprigs mint icing sugar	Garnish with the zest and mint sprigs, and dust with icing sugar.

APPLE PIE

The sweet pie is a uniquely British dish, and apples and pears were the earliest form, well established by the sixteenth century. I have altered the concept slightly, using the lighter filo pastry instead of shortcrust, and serving with a yoghurt sauce instead of cream.

Serves 10

Oven: moderate, 180°C/350°F/Gas 4

about **12** filo sheets (bought or home-made, see page 203)	Line a 30 cm (12 in) cheese cake mould with eight sheets, leaving a few for the top. Cover them all with a damp cloth.
1.4 kg (3 lb) Cox's apples, peeled and cored	Cut into quarters and finely slice. Place in a large bowl.
lemon juice to taste **100 g** (4 oz) raisins or sultanas, soaked in a little apple juice a pinch of powdered cinnamon a little sugar or warmed runny honey (optional)	Add to the bowl and mix together lightly. Fill the filo-covered mould with the apple mixture, and cover with the remaining filo sheets.
1 egg yolk	Use to glaze the top of the pie. Cook in the preheated oven for approximately 45 minutes, checking after about 20 minutes. Cover the top with foil if it colours too quickly.
275 g (10 oz) low-fat Greek yoghurt a little skimmed milk	To make a yoghurt sauce, thin the yoghurt down with a little milk. Put in a jug. Add a little cinnamon and lemon juice.
icing sugar	Just before serving, dust the surface of the pie with icing sugar and the sauce with some cinnamon.
100 g (4 oz) fresh berries mint leaves	Decorate each plate with a couple of berries and mint leaves.

TIP

A bain-marie is a roasting or baking tray half-filled with hot water in which dishes like pâtés and terrines, custards and soufflé puddings, and delicate mousselines are cooked. The water is brought to the simmer on top of the stove, then the dishes are inserted, and the whole goes into the preheated oven. The dishes are protected from fierce direct heat, cooking at the temperature of the *water*, not that of the oven (although the oven temperature is of course important, dictating whether the water in the bain-marie simmers gently or bubbles more vigorously, depending on the dish to be cooked). Bain-marie cooking also produces moisture in which the foods poach rather than bake. The addition of paper to the roasting tray protects the dish even more from the direct heat and prevents the water from boiling, which would cause the mixture to curdle. Top up if necessary with hot water, and never allow water to overflow into the dishes. The bain-marie may also be used on top of the stove.

To check that the pudding is cooked, pierce with a wooden skewer. Hold it carefully to your lips, and if it's nice and warm, the pudding is cooked.

BREAD AND BUTTER PUDDING

Dating from the early eighteenth century, this is an English nursery dish transformed. It has also become one of my best-known recipes! It's an ideal pudding to serve at a Sunday lunch – but I also serve it at dinner parties, and it's always rather well received.

Serves 10

Oven: moderate, 160°C/325°F/Gas 3

500 ml (18 fl oz) milk **500 ml** (18 fl oz) double cream a little salt **1** vanilla pod, split	Bring to the boil in a pan.
40 g (1½ oz) butter, melted	Use a little to grease a large oval pie dish.
6 large eggs **250 g** (9 oz) vanilla sugar (see page 87)	Mix together until pale, then gradually add the milk and cream mixture, stirring.
6 small soft bread rolls	Cut into thin slices and butter them. Arrange in the base of the dish.
25 g (1 oz) sultanas, soaked in water and drained	Add, along with the milk mixture, passing the latter through a sieve. The bread will float to the top. Place the dish in a bain-marie on top of folded newspaper, and pour in hot water to come halfway up the sides of the dish. Poach carefully in the preheated oven for 45–50 minutes. When the pudding is ready, it should wobble very slightly in the middle. Remove from oven and cool a little.
100 g (4 oz) apricot glaze (see page 156), warm	Brush a thin coating of glaze over the top of the pudding.
a little icing sugar	Just before serving, dust with icing sugar. Serve warm.

SUPERMARKET SHOPPING

Constant themes in my philosophy of cooking are health and the use of the best and freshest ingredients. We are all becoming much more aware of foods that are positively good for us, as well as foods that may be enjoyed in moderation. Recent nationwide figures have shown that buying trends are moving away from red meats, and towards chicken and fish. The sales of vegetables have also increased. These consumer trends are obviously interesting to those of us involved professionally in food, but they are of most significance to the large supermarket chains, who have to monitor, respond to, and even anticipate the direction in which tastes are inclining.

Supermarkets were once associated with inexpensive, swift, convenience buying, and for fresh meat, fish, vegetables, fruit, pastries, bread and charcuterie it was still necessary to visit specialist shops. Now, however, although these specialist shops still offer excellent service and products – I, as a chef and as a personal shopper, rely on them – the image of the supermarkets has changed. In the last few years, there has been a dramatic turnaround in the large stores, and in many of the chains we can expect to find the very best possible basic, fresh and good ingredients. Supermarket buyers are now in the forefront of the food revolution, searching out markets at home and abroad for the freshest, newest and best produce; often, too, the supermarkets are the means whereby we are introduced to unfamiliar and unusual foods.

In a good supermarket today you can buy everything you might need for a meal, both convenient and delicious. On offer in most supermarkets are fresh meat, poultry and fish; fresh vegetables and fruit; freshly baked breads; a wide variety of dairy produce; interesting oils, vinegars and spices; sometimes quite spectacularly innovative and inexpensive wines; and staple foods like grains, pulses and pastas. Often so much choice can be overwhelming, but the recipes in this chapter should give you the courage and confidence to choose what is best and how to assemble different ingredients for many a quick and healthy meal.

Rice, Grains and Pulses

These are the staples of most vegetarian diets, but there is absolutely no reason why others should not enjoy them as well. All contain the protein, fibre and carbohydrate required by our bodies. They must, however, be less than a year old (from the last season's crop), which should be no problem in a busy supermarket with a quick turnover.

Rice, for instance, now comes in several varieties from all

over the world – long-grain and 'wild' from North America, short-grain from Italy, basmati from India – and, in some varieties, as brown or white grains (the former nutritionally better, with nothing taken away by refining). All can be used as the simple base for vegetable, meat or seafood sauces, or cold in a salad. My own favourite rice dish is risotto (see pages 63–4).

Other grains are wheat, rye, corn, barley, millet and oats, all of which are now available in good supermarkets. They come in different guises, but many can be used in flavourful pilafs, ground into healthy flours, or eaten as cereals such as my home-made muesli on page 5.

Although the term 'pulse' strictly covers both fresh and dried peas, beans and lentils, to cooks pulses invariably mean the dried vegetable, and these retain a large proportion of the nutrients of the fresh. All that they require is a soaking in water to restore their previous moisture content before being cooked. Once again, a delicious and colourful choice is available – many types of lentils and peas, soya, bread, butter, haricot and flageolet beans, to name but a few. They too can be cooked in meat or vegetable sauces, or served cold in salads.

Sprouting Grains, Seeds and Pulses

Sprouts are a very nourishing food, and you can now often find them in good supermarkets or health-food shops. Sprouts contain less carbohydrates (used to provide energy for growing), therefore less calories than their 'bean' counterparts, and more vitamin C. They are nutritionally midway between the vegetable and the dormant seed; easier to digest, and fresher than most vegetables for the city-dweller. They taste good – nutty, crisp and juicy – as well as look good, with their curling shapes and fronds on salads. They are most nutritious when the seed is still attached to the tiny sprout.

The types of sprouts most available for buying are those of mung and soya beans (the former the ones used by the Chinese), and alfalfa seeds (tiny and very nutritious). But other seeds, grains and pulses may be sprouted at home for a variety of healthy tastes. Try adzuki beans, buckwheat, corn, chickpeas, fenugreek seeds (an ingredient of some curry powders, and the sprouts have a distinctly spicy flavour), all types of lentils, sesame seeds and wheat. You must, however, buy them whole and *untreated*, or they will not sprout at all. See page 66 for instructions.

Chicken

It's good to see more and more fresh, free-range chickens available in this country, and supermarkets have been partly responsible for this. Chicken is now one of the nation's most popular foods, principally because it's fairly inexpensive, low in fat, high in protein and quick and easy to cook.

Chickens are known by a variety of names according to their methods of rearing, age and weight. A favourite of mine is the delicate-fleshed poussin, the smallest and youngest, which weigh 300–700 g (11 oz–1½ lb). Larger chickens of six to eight weeks old include those which are corn or maize fed; this gives them a yellow colour and a unique flavour, and simply roasted or baked (see pages 80 and 134) they are quite exceptional. Smoked chickens are becoming increasingly available, and these are very useful to serve with or in salads, or even warmed through a little as in the recipe on page 81.

Exotic Fruits, Vegetables and Flavourings

More information on the exotics is now available, and many of the supermarkets have themselves published leaflets on unusual fruits and vegetables. I thrive on the increasing choice. Vegetables like kohlrabi, celeriac, fennel, sweet potatoes, wild mushrooms and aubergines, are all now seen in their seasons, and can be used in many delicious ways. Yam, for instance – large tubers of vine-like plants – can be cooked as in the recipe on page 129.

Baby vegetables, the product of a new trend which I welcome, are bursting with flavour, ideal to use as garnishes or in stir-fries – aubergines or egg plants, sweetcorn, leeks, courgettes and cherry tomatoes.

There is a vast choice in supermarkets of fruits once only to be found in expensive specialist or ethnic shops. Mangoes, papayas (pawpaws), kiwi fruit, lychees and pineapples have become almost as common as apples and pears, and they are best eaten or enjoyed by themselves simply as fruit, but from time to time they may be transformed into wonderful desserts. Less familiar fruits such as carambola, guava and babaco are also appearing on the shelves of enlightened supermarkets, and these too are delicious. Passion fruit, for instance, despite their wrinkled, unprepossessing appearance, contain a flesh which is quite amazingly pungent and fragrant, and I use them in a soufflé for special parties (see page 187). My favourite way with exotic fruits, though, is as a selection of purées (see page 84).

Flavourings from afar are also offered by supermarkets now – in one brief excursion through a northern store, I came across lemongrass, blades of a grass used mainly in South-East Asian cookery for a lemony fragrance, and tamarind, a pod whose sour flesh is used as an acidic all over India, the Caribbean and parts of the Middle East.

With Kit Chan, preparing salads with the best of the morning's fresh supermarket produce

Salads

Because of my constant emphasis on healthy foods I suppose it must come as no surprise that I am a great salad enthusiast. In this country, salad is still often thought of as a summer lettuce dish, with or without dressing, or as a dietary penance. However, with the recent strides forward in knowledge about healthy foods – particularly raw foods – and the increasingly wonderful lettuce types grown, this attitude is radically changing. Take a look around the shelves of your supermarket and you will find radiccio, oakleaf and lamb's lettuce, Chinese leaves, spinach, sorrel, endive and chicory. These can immediately form the basis of a quick and nutritious meal, and provide a welcome contrast of bitterness, sweetness and textures. Use these leaves in combination with many other ingredients – nuts, cheese, vegetables, fruit, sprouted seeds or beans, or beans, rice and other grains. Anything that is colourful, of a good texture, and that will *do* you good, can be used. You will find quite a selection to choose from in the following pages.

I hope that I have opened your eyes to the treasures you can find in your local supermarket, if that type of shopping appeals to you, and is more convenient. I also hope that you will wander around the shelves in the future with a fresh awareness of what can be transformed with ease into quick, nutritious and delicious meals.

61

Risotto

Risotto is one of the most versatile dishes you can prepare as, once you have mastered the simple basic technique of cooking it, you can add a multitude of flavourings – and all of these will be available at some time in your supermarket.

The first necessity, of course, is the right kind of rice. Because risotto is so uniquely Italian, only Italian rice will do. This is grown in the valley of the Po, the most important rice-growing area in Europe, and there are several varieties. Best are *vialone* and *arborio*, the latter more readily available in shops other than specialist Italian delicatessens. *Arborio* has a fat round grain which absorbs liquid slowly, leaving it soft and sticky outside but still with a hint of *al dente* bite in the middle – exactly what one wants with risotto.

Another necessity for risotto is a good stock, and you will find a choice of stocks on pages 192–6. The stock should always match the principal flavouring addition of the risotto – chicken for chicken, fish for fish etc. Good quality Parmesan cheese is another vital element of most risottos, and a little, freshly grated from the piece, is added (sometimes with some butter), towards the end of cooking time. More cheese is then sprinkled over each serving to taste. (This Swiss use Sbrinz instead of Parmesan.)

A good risotto is not too difficult to make, but it does require patience and dedication. It is not a rice pilaff, nor is it boiled rice, both of which can be left to their own devices. Risotto needs to be stood over, stirred and cajoled into the right state of moist, slightly sticky, readiness. Treat the rice grains like gold dust, with love, care and feeling.

On the next page is one recipe for a courgette risotto, but there are any number of flavourings and ingredients that can be added: grated Parmesan alone, bone marrow and saffron (risotto Milanese, the perfect accompaniment for an *osso-buco*), wild mushrooms (as in the photograph opposite), asparagus, young spring vegetables (the risotto *primavera* so beloved in Venice), chicken livers, meat sauce, clams . . .

A risotto makes a good start to a meal (or it can of course be served as a main course), but it should be eaten as soon as it is cooked, just as a soufflé should be. It should never be allowed to stand once cooked, nor should it be reheated.

Left: Courgette and Thyme Risotto (page 64). *Right:* Wild Mushroom Risotto

COURGETTE AND THYME RISOTTO

Serves 4–6

25 g (1 oz) butter	Melt in a suitable pan.
1 small onion, finely chopped **1** sprig fresh thyme	Add, and cook gently without colouring for about 2–3 minutes.
200 g (7 oz) *arborio* rice a pinch of turmeric	Add, stirring to coat the rice thoroughly with butter, using a wooden spoon. Do not let anything brown.
approx **400 ml** (14 fl oz) simmering white stock (vegetable or chicken, see pages 192 and 193)	Add about 150 ml (¼ pint), and begin stirring. The rice will immediately start to become creamy (as the starch is released). Over a medium heat keep adding stock in similar small quantities to retain that creamy consistency as the rice absorbs the stock.
250 g (9 oz) small courgettes, trimmed and cubed	Add and stir continually, adding gradually less stock, until the rice is ready (soft outside but with an inner firmness), which will take about 15 minutes altogether.
50 ml (2 fl oz) dry white wine	Add just a few seconds before you judge the rice to be ready. This stops the cooking. Remove from heat.
butter (optional) freshly grated Parmesan cheese salt and freshly ground pepper	Stir in a knob of butter if you like, with some grated Parmesan to taste, and taste for seasoning (the stock should have flavoured the rice, and the cheese if fairly salty). Serve immediately with a separate bowl of Parmesan cheese from which guests can help themselves.

SALADS AND DRESSINGS

Whatever the constituents of your salads, dress them carefully and with love, matching flavours and textures. There are many oils and vinegars available (some you can 'make' yourself, see pages 205 and 206), as well as other ingredients such as cheese and yoghurt. You acquire a 'feel' for dressings to go with different salads, and you'll find many suggestions on the following pages. Generally the proportion of oil to mild vinegar is two parts to one, but sometimes, especially with a delicate leaf salad (which could collapse if the oil content was too high), I use more vinegar. I like particularly the combination of balsamic vinegar and olive oil; sherry vinegar makes a good marriage with hazelnut and walnut too. Vegetable salads, for instance, can take a bit of creaminess (although I would use yoghurt, quark or fromage frais instead of cream itself), and a salad made from large juicy Mediterranean tomatoes sometimes needs little more than a sprinkling of the very best olive oil, and a scattering of shredded basil.

Never forget about *herbs* in salads (nor, of course, in any other aspect of cookery): basil, parsley, thyme, fennel, dill, sage, marjoram and oregano, and leaves like watercress, sorrel and rocket, make their own unique contribution to many salad combinations.

Do not dress a salad until the very last minute, and a large bowl is necessary so that leaves don't end up on the floor as you mix the ingredients. Never use metal cutlery as this can tear salad ingredients, but use wooden spoons, or your clean hand.

CHICKEN AND NOODLE SALAD

Serves 4

450 g (1 lb) fresh multicoloured noodles (see page 203)	Cook, drain and allow to cool.
200 g (7 oz) smoked or roasted chicken meat	Cut into suitably sized pieces.
30 ml (2 tbsp) chopped parsley **60 ml** (2½ fl oz) balsamic vinegar **125 ml** (4½ fl oz) olive oil	To make the parsley vinaigrette, blend together in a liquidiser.
salt and freshly ground pepper	Season to taste.
30 ml (2 tbsp) freshly grated Parmesan cheese	Either mix the noodles with the dressing, garnish with the chicken and sprinkle with the Parmesan, or mix everything together.

CHINESE LEAF SALAD

Serves 4

450 g (1 lb) Chinese leaves	Shred.
225 g (8 oz) soya bean sprouts.	Pick over and wash. Drain well.
30 ml (2 tbsp) nut oil **15 ml** (1 tbsp) finely chopped fresh ginger **1** clove garlic, finely chopped	Heat the oil in a wide pan or wok, and add the ginger and garlic. Sweat for a few minutes to release their flavours. Toss in the sprouts and shredded leaves and stir around very briefly to coat them with the oil and flavourings. Remove from heat and place in a large bowl.
¼ red pepper, cleaned and finely chopped **25 g** (1 oz) spring onions, cut into fine strips **50 g** (2 oz) unsalted peanuts	Add.
a dash of light soy sauce **1** lime, juiced salt and freshly ground pepper	Season salad to taste. Toss and serve.

TIP

For sprouts, simply put a handful of your chosen seed, grain or pulse into a large glass jar, cover with lukewarm water and leave for about 12 hours. Cover the jar with a piece of muslin and attach with a rubber band. Pour the water from the jar through the cloth, and then put the jar in a dry dark place for germination to begin. Rinse the seeds once or twice a day with fresh lukewarm water, draining them well, and in three to six days, depending on type, you will have sprouts of varying lengths. Swill well in water to rid them of husks – and use in salads, stir-fries or simply as a healthy snack. You can also buy a sprouting-box.

Clockwise: Carrot, Orange and Date Salad (page 76); Warm Vegetable Salad (page 78); Red Cabbage, Sultana and Apple Salad (below)

RED CABBAGE, SULTANA AND APPLE SALAD

Serves 4

1 small red cabbage, shredded **5 ml** (1 tsp) salt	Place the cabbage in a large bowl and sprinkle with salt. Let sit for 15–20 minutes, then wash and drain well. Replace in the rinsed salad bowl.
2 apples, washed, cored and cut into cubes **50 g** (2 oz) sultanas, soaked for 15 minutes	Add to the cabbage.
salt and freshly ground pepper a pinch of sugar **25 ml** (1 fl oz) cider vinegar **50 ml** (2 fl oz) grapeseed oil	Make a vinaigrette by dissolving some salt, pepper and sugar to taste in the vinegar, then mixing in the oil. Pour over the salad and mix in immediately before the apple browns.

Above: Chicken and Noodle Salad (page 65). *Below:* Lentil Salad Melanie (opposite)

MIXED LEAF SALAD

Serves 4

200 g (7 oz) prepared salad leaves (radiccio, lollo rosso, endive, frisée, oakleaf, lamb's lettuce etc)	Mix together in a suitable bowl.
15 ml (1 tbsp) Dijon mustard salt and freshly ground pepper **10 ml** (2 tsp) sherry vinegar **5–10 ml** (1–2 tsp) walnut oil **30 ml** (2 tbsp) olive oil **10 ml** (2 tsp) balsamic vinegar	To make the dressing, place the mustard in a small bowl with the salt and pepper. Slowly add the sherry vinegar drop by drop, and mix well. Add the oils slowly, whisking all the time, then stir in the balsamic vinegar. Pour the dressing over the salad and toss well. Arrange on four plates.
30 ml (2 tbsp) finely snipped chives	Sprinkle over the salad.

LENTIL SALAD MELANIE

Serves 4

100 g (4 oz) green lentil sprouts **100 g** (4 oz) red lentil sprouts **50 g** (2 oz) wheat sprouts	Rinse well and drain.
100 g (4 oz) cherry tomatoes **20 g** (¾ oz) spring onion, finely cut	Mix with the sprouts in a suitable bowl.
5 g (¼ oz) fresh yeast **1** small clove garlic, crushed **10 ml** (2 tsp) white wine vinegar **100 g** (4 oz) plain yoghurt **5 g** (¼ oz) fresh dill and parsley, finely chopped **10 ml** (2 tsp) grain mustard **10 ml** (2 tsp) soy sauce salt and freshly ground pepper	For the yeast dressing, mix everything in another bowl, and beat together, using a whisk. Season to taste. Pour over the salad and toss.

MEDITERRANEAN TOMATO SALAD WITH FETA CHEESE AND BASIL

Serves 4

2 Mediterranean (or beef) tomatoes	Remove the stem and core, and cut into slices approximately 3 mm (⅛ in) thick. Arrange the slices on a large serving plate.
200 g (7 oz) Feta cheese	Cut into 1 cm (½ in) cubes and place on top.
salt and freshly ground pepper olive oil	Lightly season and sprinkle with a little olive oil.
1 small bunch fresh basil leaves	Tear into fine strips and scatter over the top of the salad.

TIP
Buy the tomatoes a few days in advance to ripen them well. Feta is often quite strong in flavour – you can use other cheeses, like goat cheese, instead.

SALADE FANTAISIE

Serves 4

1 lettuce	Carefully wash, then tear into bite-sized pieces, and drain in a sieve.
300 g (11 oz) oranges	Peel, slice fairly thickly and cut into cubes, retaining four slices for decoration.
1 small red onion, peeled and sliced into rings **100 g** (4 oz) stuffed olives, sliced	Place in a large bowl, and add the drained lettuce and orange cubes.
150 g (5 oz) plain yoghurt **45 ml** (3 tbsp) olive oil **30 ml** (2 tbsp) fruit vinegar (raspberry, etc, see page 206) **15 ml** (1 tbsp) soy sauce **5 ml** (1 tsp) honey **5 ml** (1 tsp) herb mustard salt and freshly ground pepper	Make a dressing by whisking together the yoghurt, oil and vinegar first, then mixing in the remaining ingredients. Toss the salad with the dressing, then decorate with the orange slices.
15 ml (1 tbsp) finely chopped parsley **40 g** (1½ oz) shelled walnuts, chopped	Sprinkle over the salad.

TIP
When using raw onion in fresh salads, you can remove some of the pungency by soaking in a little salted water for 15 minutes. Drain and soak in fresh water for a further 10 minutes. Rinse and drain well.

MIXED VEGETABLE SALAD

Serves 4

1 large kohlrabi, peeled salt	Cut into shapes that approximate those of the mangetout and sweetcorn. Plunge into boiling, lightly salted water and blanch for about 30 seconds. Drain, then refresh in cold water, and dry.
50 g (2 oz) mangetout, topped and tailed **100 g** (4 oz) baby sweetcorn, trimmed	Blanch separately in the same boiling water for about 30 seconds. Drain, refresh as above, and dry.
1 red pepper, cleaned and cut into strips	Put with the blanched vegetables into a large bowl.
10 ml (2 tsp) grain mustard **150 g** (5 oz) plain yoghurt **30 ml** (2 tbsp) red wine vinegar salt and freshly ground pepper	Mix together, adding salt and pepper to taste. Pour over the salad ingredients and toss. Serve immediately.

TIP
Kohlrabi, a brassica not unlike broccoli stalk in flavour, is now to be found quite easily; popular in Europe, it was unknown here until lately. When young and full of flavour, I like to use it, lightly blanched, in salads.

FENNEL, RAISIN AND WALNUT SALAD

Serves 4

100 g (4 oz) walnuts, shelled	Blanch briefly in boiling water, to remove the skins. Drain and dry, and place in a bowl.
50 g (2 oz) raisins	Soak in water for about 10 minutes to make them plump and juicy. Then drain, dry, and add to the bowl.
2 medium fennel bulbs	Cut in half from top to bottom and remove and discard the hard central cores. Finely slice the crisp flesh and put in the bowl. Retain the feathery tops for the garnish.
salt and freshly ground pepper **25 ml** (1 fl oz) sherry vinegar **50 ml** (2 fl oz) olive oil	Dissolve salt and pepper to taste in the vinegar, then stir in the olive oil and mix into the salad ingredients in the bowl.
2 heads chicory (Belgian endive) paprika	Separate the leaves and dip each point in paprika. Arrange like vertical petals around the bowl of salad, paprika side up. Sprinkle the fennel tops over the whole salad.

Clockwise: Spinach, Bacon and
Croûton Salad (opposite);
Couscous Salad (page 149);
Mediterranean Tomato Salad with
Feta Cheese and Basil (page 70)

SPINACH, BACON AND CROÛTON SALAD

Serves 4	**Oven**: moderately hot, 200°C/400°F/Gas 6
225 g (8 oz) fresh young spinach leaves, thick stalks removed	Wash in several changes of cold water, and leave to drain thoroughly.
75 g (3 oz) day-old bread, crusts removed and cut into small croûtons, or a small French loaf, sliced thinly	Lay on an oven tray. Bake in the oven for about 10 minutes until golden.
1 clove garlic, crushed	Add to the croûtons, and mix to flavour.
100 g (4 oz) bacon chop, rind removed	Chop into 1 cm (½ in) dice and fry until crisp. Remove dice from pan.
30 ml (2 tbsp) wine vinegar	Pour into the pan and mix with the (minimal) bacon fat. Put the spinach, bacon and croûtons in a large bowl, and dress with the vinegar and bacon fat. Eat straightaway.

Variation

Stilton dressing
Instead of using bacon, bacon fat and vinegar, the salad can be served with this dressing. Mix 30 ml (2 tbsp) lemon juice with 15 ml (1 tbsp) Dijon mustard and 150 g (5 oz) plain low-fat yoghurt. Soften 40 g (1½ oz) Stilton (at room temperature) with a fork and mix in, with some pepper to taste. Garnish with 25 g (1 oz) rinded Stilton, cut into cubes.

CARROT, ORANGE AND DATE SALAD

Serves 4

100 g (4 oz) curly endive, washed and dried	Divide between individual plates.
250 g (9 oz) carrots, peeled and coarsely grated **2 oranges**, segmented (see page 6) **100 g** (4 oz) fresh dates (if available, otherwise dried), split in half and stoned	Mix and place on top of the bed of leaves.
salt and freshly ground pepper	Lightly season to taste.
30 ml (2 tbsp) white wine vinegar or cider vinegar the juices from the orange segmenting **75 ml** (5 tbsp) grapeseed oil **2.5 ml** (½ tsp) Dijon mustard	Mix together and pour over salad. Toss well, and serve.

COLOURFUL POTATO SALAD

Serves 4

200 g (7 oz) plain low-fat yoghurt	Pour into a large paper filter (or paper towel, folded) in a sieve, and leave to drain.
400 g (14 oz) early or new potatoes, scrubbed	Cook in their skins for 15–20 minutes, or until nearly done, then peel while still warm, and dice.
1 medium cucumber salt	Cut into strips lengthwise and then dice, sprinkle lightly with salt and put to one side to drain in a sieve.
1 egg, hard-boiled	Peel and chop.
300 g (11 oz) firm, fleshy tomatoes, washed	Cut into quarters, spoon out the core and seeds, and then dice the flesh.
1 bunch spring onions	Clean and cut into fine rings.
1 bunch radishes, washed	Cut into quarters.

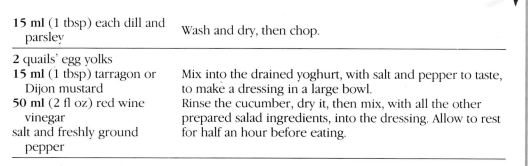

15 ml (1 tbsp) each dill and parsley	Wash and dry, then chop.
2 quails' egg yolks **15 ml** (1 tbsp) tarragon or Dijon mustard **50 ml** (2 fl oz) red wine vinegar salt and freshly ground pepper	Mix into the drained yoghurt, with salt and pepper to taste, to make a dressing in a large bowl. Rinse the cucumber, dry it, then mix, with all the other prepared salad ingredients, into the dressing. Allow to rest for half an hour before eating.

KIDNEY BEAN SALAD

Serves 4

100 g (4 oz) red kidney beans **100 g** (4 oz) white kidney beans	Cover separately with cold water, bring to the boil and boil for 10 minutes. Turn the heat off and leave to soak for 2 hours. Then drain both pots, cover separately with fresh cold water, and boil gently for about 1½–2 hours, or until the beans are tender. Refresh with cold water and drain well, then leave to cool in a bowl.
100 g (4 oz) thick sliced ham, roughly cubed **50 g** (2 oz) Spanish onion, finely chopped **5 ml** (1 tsp) finely chopped parsley	Add to the beans.
salt and freshly ground pepper	Season to taste.
80 ml (3¼ fl oz) olive oil **50 ml** (2 fl oz) red wine vinegar	Mix together, and dress the salad, tossing well.

TIP
Never add salt to dried beans while cooking as this toughens their skins. Add only when they are cooked.

WARM VEGETABLE SALAD

Serves 4

1 medium red pepper **1** medium yellow pepper	Skin as described on page 150, then cut into 2 cm (¾ in) cubes.
1 medium onion, peeled	Cut into fine slices.
4 medium courgettes, topped and tailed	Cut into slices or wedges.
60 ml (4 tbsp) sesame oil	Heat in a wok or frying pan.
1 small clove garlic, crushed **1** sprig thyme **10** coriander seeds, crushed	Add, and stir-fry with the onion for a minute, before adding the courgettes, then the red and yellow peppers.
salt and freshly ground pepper	Season to taste, and let the mixture cook for about 2–3 minutes. It should still be crunchy. Remove from heat.
30 ml (2 tbsp) sherry vinegar	Stir in, and leave the mixture to marinate for a while. Serve warm.

YOGHURT BASIL DRESSING

Make the light summery dressing about two hours before you want to use it, as this allows all the flavours to blend.

Makes about 500 ml (18 fl oz)

salt and freshly ground pepper **15 ml** (1 tbsp) sugar **60 ml** (4 tbsp) Dijon mustard	Place in a bowl and whisk together.
250 g (9 oz) plain yoghurt	Add, and mix to a creamy texture.
50 ml (2 fl oz) sunflower oil **125 ml** (4½ fl oz) red wine vinegar	Gradually pour in, whisking continuously.
at least **15 ml** (1 tbsp) fresh basil, finely sliced	Add just before serving. Season to taste.

HERB VINAIGRETTE

When making a vinaigrette, always add the seasonings to the acid (the vinegar or lemon juice) first. If you mix the oil, acid and seasonings together at the same time, the oil covers the spices like a coat, and they will not be distributed evenly.

Makes about 200 ml (7 fl oz)

30 ml (2 tbsp) red wine or sherry vinegar salt and freshly ground pepper	Mix in a bowl, seasoning to taste.
90 ml (6 tbsp) olive oil, slightly warmed	Add, very slowly and gradually at first, mixing with a whisk.
45 ml (3 tbsp) finely chopped fresh herbs (parsley, chives, tarragon, chervil, basil) **30 ml (2 tbsp) diced** tomatoes	Add, just before serving, mixing in well.

THOUSAND ISLAND DRESSING

All the ingredients should be at a warm room temperature so that the dressing does not curdle. Keep in the refrigerator.

Makes about 500 ml (18 fl oz)

2 egg yolks, hard-boiled and sieved **80 ml (3¼ fl oz) sherry** vinegar or lemon juice salt and ground pepper	Mix together in a bowl, adding seasoning to taste.
250 ml (9 fl oz) olive oil	Mix in, a drop at a time, with a whisk.
45 ml (3 tbsp) chilli sauce **15–30 ml (1–2 tbsp)** brandy	Mix in.
125 ml (4½ fl oz) whipping cream, whipped, or plain yoghurt, drained	Fold in.
1 small red pepper, cleaned and finely chopped a pinch of paprika	Just before serving, add the pepper, and season with paprika and some more salt if necessary.

ROAST CHICKEN WITH GARLIC AND ROSEMARY

Nothing is more delicious than a good, roasted chicken, and the best are the corn- or maize-fed birds now so freely available in good supermarkets, with their glorious yellow flesh. Cook them really simply to enjoy them at their best, roasted as here, or baked in a clay pot as on page 134.

Serves 4	**Oven:** moderately hot, 200°C/400°F/Gas 6
1 corn-fed chicken, about 1.4 kg (3 lb) salt and freshly ground pepper	Clean and season inside and outside.
1 clove garlic, lightly crushed with skin **2** sprigs rosemary	Place in the cavity.
40 ml (1½ fl oz) olive oil	Place the chicken on a greased roasting tin and brush with oil. Roast in the preheated oven for about 20 minutes per 450 g (1 lb), basting occasionally, and covering with oiled greaseproof paper or foil if the breast is becoming too brown. Remove from the oven and allow to rest for a few minutes before carving. Eat warm, with salads of choice.

WARM SMOKED CHICKEN

Smoked chicken is a fairly new item in supermarkets – and, occasionally, good butchers – and they have a wonderful flavour. The most obvious usage is cold in a salad (see page 65), but here it is warm, and served with a selection of seasonal vegetables.

Serves 4

Ingredients	Method
1 large smoked chicken, about 800 g–1 kg (1¾–2¼ lb) 20 g (¾ oz) butter	Remove the backbone and wing tips and brown lightly in the butter in a large pan. Meanwhile, joint the chicken neatly into eight pieces and set aside.
1.5 litres (2½ pints) strong chicken stock (see page 193)	Pour into the pan with the browned bones and bring to the boil, skimming occasionally. Lower the heat, cover and simmer for 15 minutes, skimming as required. Strain, then return the stock to the rinsed-out pan and continue to simmer until it is reduced considerably.
30 ml (2 tbsp) vegetable oil about 300 g (11 oz) selected vegetables (yellow or green beans, courgettes, carrots, leeks, small mushrooms, beansprouts) 1 garlic clove 1 sprig thyme	Heat the oil gently in a deep wide pan. Cut courgettes, carrots and leeks into strips. Sweat the vegetables (except mushrooms if using) with the garlic and thyme, without allowing to colour. Pour in the reduced stock and simmer for 5–6 minutes. Add the chicken and mushrooms and cook gently until warmed through.
salt and freshly ground pepper 4 sprigs fresh basil	Season and garnish with fresh basil.

HERB-STEAMED POUSSINS

Bear garlic – *Allium ursinum* or ramson – is a member of the lily family to which leeks, onions and garlic belong, and is quite widespread in the wild in Europe. The smell is powerfully garlicky, but it diminishes on cooking. It is a herb used medicinally on the Continent, as indeed is garlic itself, long known for its therapeutic properties.

Serves 4

4 poussins, about 400 g (14 oz) each ½ clove garlic 40 g (1½ oz) butter, softened	Rub the poussins all over with the garlic, then smear with the butter.
1 bunch coriander, leaves shredded, stems reserved	Very gently loosen the skin covering the breasts and insert the coriander leaves.
salt and freshly ground pepper 40 g (1½ oz) bear garlic leaves	Season the poussins lightly, and wrap in the leaves. Line a steaming basket with foil and place the poussins on top.
1 small piece fresh root ginger, cut into julienne strips	Scatter over the poussins and set aside.
1 litre (1¾ pints) chicken stock (see page 193) 1 lemon, juiced 2 shallots, sliced	In the base of the steamer bring to the boil together, along with the coriander stalks. Continue to boil until reduced to 600 ml (1 pint). Place the basket on top, cover and simmer for about 15 minutes.
½ cucumber, peeled, seeded and sliced 2 tomatoes, quartered and seeded	Add to the steamer and continue to cook for a further 3–5 minutes until the poussins are tender and the vegetables cooked.
4 sprigs flat-leaved parsley or coriander	Garnish with herbs. If you wish, you can serve some of the stock as a sauce to accompany the poussins.

FRESH FRUIT PURÉES

Fruit purées are easy to prepare, and they're very healthy, packed with fibre and vitamin C. With the huge selection of delicious fruit from near and far now available in our supermarkets, a virtually instantaneous dessert can be made at any time of the year. Vary your ingredients accordingly. I could have used blackcurrants, apples or pears, for instance. Most fruits have their own natural sugar; if not sweet enough, add a little sugar to the purées.

Serves 4

400 g (14 oz) mangoes, peeled, stoned and chopped ½ lemon, juiced	Blend in the liquidiser with a little of the lemon juice, and push through a sieve into a bowl.
250 g (9 oz) ripe melon, peeled and seeded **200 g** (7 oz) strawberries, cleaned **150 g** (5 oz) raspberries **200 g** (7 oz) papaya, peeled and seeded **225 g** (8 oz) kiwi fruit, peeled	Do exactly the same as above, *separately*, with all the fruit. Put all the bowls into the refrigerator and chill.
100 ml (4 fl oz) mineral water, chilled	To serve, bring the fruit bowls out, and thin down any if necessary with a little mineral water. You need all the purées to have the same consistency. They should spread slowly when poured. Put a scoop of each fruit purée on to a plate, arranging them around the plate so that the magnificent colours contrast well.
60 ml (4 tbsp) runny plain yoghurt	Put a spoonful in the centre of the fruit purées. Give the plate a fairly firm knock on a solid surface to settle the purées and blend them together at the edges. Then draw a thin wooden skewer through the purées in a light pattern.
icing sugar **2** large strawberries, halved **4** sprigs fresh mint	Sprinkle with a little icing sugar and decorate each plate with a half strawberry and a mint sprig.

EXOTIC FRUIT TERRINE WITH RASPBERRY SAUCE

The fruit terrine idea is a basic of Cuisine Naturelle, using only the natural sweetness of the fruits and pure fruit juices.

Serves 15

8 leaves gelatine, soaked in cold water and squeezed dry **300 ml** (½ pint) pure orange juice **100 ml** (4 fl oz) clear apple juice	Dissolve gelatine in a little of the mixed fruit juices, warmed. Add the remaining juice and leave to cool. Surround a large china or glass terrine dish – at least 1.5 litres (2½ pints) – with ice. Pour a little of the juice on the base. Allow to set.
1 bunch fresh peppermint leaves	Arrange some peppermint leaves over the jelly. Turn the terrine on to its side, and coat that side with a little of the juice. Allow to set and arrange mint leaves over. Repeat on the other three sides.
2 large mangoes, peeled, stoned and sliced **30** lychees, peeled, halved and stoned **2** large papayas, peeled, seeded and sliced **8** figs, trimmed and sliced	Place the fruit in layers in the terrine, pouring a little of the juice over each layer of fruit, and allowing it to set before continuing with the next layer. When all the fruit and juice is in, chill the terrine for 2–3 hours until set.
300 g (11 oz) raspberries **30 ml** (2 tbsp) icing sugar **1** small lemon, juiced	To make the raspberry sauce, purée then strain the raspberries, and mix with the sugar and lemon juice. Chill. When ready to serve, turn the terrine out carefully on to a dish by dipping the base and sides briefly into hot water to loosen. Slice neatly and serve with the raspberry sauce.
mint sprigs	Decorate with mint sprigs.

TIP
Basically any seasonal fruit, exotic or otherwise, can be used for this terrine – except for pineapple and kiwi fruit, which contain enzymes that prevent gelatine from setting. (These can be inactivated by simmering the fruit, or another solution would be to use agar agar, a vegetable 'gelatine', instead of conventional gelatine.)

PINEAPPLE SURPRISE

If a pineapple is ripe, it will have fresh, lively and stiff plumes of leaves. A leaf should pull out easily, it should *smell* of pineapple, and it should feel a little soft.

Serves 4

1 large (or 4 baby) pineapple(s)	Cut the plume top off the pineapple(s) and scoop out the flesh, leaving a shell. Dice half the flesh and purée the rest (about 300 g/11 oz flesh).
125 g (4½ oz) sugar	Cook both dice and purée in a pan with 75 g (3 oz) of the sugar for 6–7 minutes, then cool.
2 egg yolks	Meanwhile, for the basic ice-cream custard mix, cream together the egg yolks and the remaining sugar, then place in the top of a double boiler.
200 ml (7 fl oz) milk **150 ml** (¼ pint) double cream ¼ vanilla pod	Bring to the boil in a pan. Add the hot liquid gradually to the egg yolk mixture and, stirring all the time, place the double boiler back on the heat. Simmer very gently and stir until the mixture coats the back of a wooden spoon. Leave to cool. Stir the pineapple into the custard, and freeze until creamy. To serve, spoon or pipe the pineapple ice-cream into the pineapple shell(s), and put the plume top back on. Serve immediately.

TIPS

Vanilla is the pod of a climbing orchid native to Central America, and was used for flavouring chocolate by the Aztecs. It is always best used in the pod form for the true flavour. Although pods are expensive to buy, they can be used again and again; after simmering in milk or whatever, carefully wash and dry and store for the next time. A simpler technique, as vanilla is invariably used in sweet dishes, is to store the pods in a jar of sugar to which they will impart their flavour. Synthetic vanilla is crude in comparison; always look for 'pure' essence or extract, which will have originated with the real thing.

Left: Baby Pineapple with Exotic Fruit Salad (page 88). *Right:* Pineapple Surprise | (above)

M

BABY PINEAPPLE WITH EXOTIC FRUIT SALAD

Often small or baby pineapples are much nicer and more sensible for the home cook, as the giant ones seem to ripen so unevenly.

Serves 4

4 baby pineapples	Prepare the pineapple shells as in the previous recipe. Cut the scooped-out flesh into 5 cm (2 in) cubes.
1 papaya 1 mango 2 kiwi fruit	Peel, stone and pip as appropriate, and cut flesh into 5 cm (2 in) cubes.
4 passion fruit a dash of rum (optional)	Cut in half and scoop out fleshy seeds. Mix with a little rum if desired.
icing sugar to dust	Fill the pineapple with the mixture, garnish with a pineapple leaf, and dust with icing sugar.

COCONUT ICE-CREAM

If you can't get a fresh coconut, use the equivalent weight of desiccated coconut. Soak it in 300 ml (½ pint) boiling water until cold, then use the meat and 50 ml (2 fl oz) of the soaking liquid as below.

Serves 4

1 fresh coconut	Crack open carefully so that you can save the milk. Remove 100 g (4 oz) of the meat, shred it roughly and place in a pan.
2 egg yolks 150 g (5 oz) caster sugar	Mix well together, then add to the coconut meat.
200 ml (7 fl oz) milk 200 ml (7 fl oz) double cream	Heat together with 50 ml (2 fl oz) of the coconut milk, and add gradually to the coconut and egg yolks, stirring. Bring the mixture slowly to just below boiling point, stirring constantly. Immediately remove from the heat and place the pan in a bain-marie of cold water, stirring occasionally until it is cold. Strain through a fine sieve, and freeze. Serve in half coconut shells or appropriate glasses.

TIP
To check that a coconut is fresh, shake it. There should be a reassuring swish of the milk inside.

PISTACHIO ICE-CREAM

Serves 4

120 g (4¼ oz) shelled pistachio nuts **130 g** (4½ oz) caster sugar	Finely grind nuts with some of the sugar in a processor.
200 ml (7 fl oz) milk	Put in a pan with the nuts and bring to the boil.
200 ml (7 fl oz) double cream **2** egg yolks	Mix with the remaining sugar in a bowl, then pour in some of the hot nut milk. Mix well, then pour the egg yolk mixture into the bulk of the nut milk. Put back over heat, and stir continuously until it comes back to the boil and rises in the pan. Remove immediately from the heat, pass the mixture through a sieve, then allow to cool.
100 ml (4 fl oz) Maraschino	Add, then freeze.

GINGER ICE WITH MANGO

A highly flavoured ice which is served with strips of mango – and a tiny amount of chocolate sauce.

Serves 4

200 ml (7 fl oz) milk	Bring to the boil.
75 g (3 oz) caster sugar **2** egg yolks **60 ml** (4 tbsp) ginger syrup (from the ginger jar)	Mix together in a basin over a pan of simmering water. Pour the hot milk on to the egg mixture, stirring well, and whisk until pale and frothy. Allow to become cold.
3 pieces stem ginger, finely diced **200 g** (7 oz) plain yoghurt	Fold in. Freeze, then when half frozen, beat well and return to the freezer until required.
20 g (¾ oz) caster sugar **100 ml** (4 fl oz) water **60 g** (2½ oz) good plain chocolate, broken into pieces	To make the chocolate sauce, dissolve the sugar and water together over gentle heat. Add the chocolate to the sugar syrup, and whisk until it melts. Simmer for about 7 minutes until the sauce is thickened and shiny. Cool.
1 ripe mango, peeled and cut into strips	To serve, arrange a fan of mango strips on a plate with a scoop of ice-cream. Pour a little chocolate sauce on the plate.
12 wild strawberries	Decorate with wild strawberries.

M

FISH

You may have heard me say it before: fish is what I like to cook and eat most. There is an endless variety of fish and seafood types, with different flavours and textures, and an almost infinite number of ways in which to cook them. I have been catching and cooking fish since boyhood, and I'm still inspired by it now – getting up with boundless enthusiasm at daybreak to 'catch' the best bargains at the market, whether at home or abroad.

Always look to see what is on sale before you make the final choice of recipe, when cooking fish. It's a mistake to decide on a particular fish when it may not be available or at its best. Often a recipe for one fish may be adapted for another of the same category or family (one of the delights of fish cookery, it's very flexible), but it is still best to look, judge and feel (if you can) before making up your mind. Never hesitate to ask your fishmonger's advice either; if he is good at his job, he will be delighted to point you in the right direction. You may be hesitant about a fish that you have never bought (or indeed seen) before – how to cook it, what would go well with it – but basically fish cookery is very simple. If the fish is fresh and in perfect condition, it will need little more than some oil or butter, some seasoning, and a few herbs.

When cooking fish – and also when choosing an alternative fish to cook in a recipe – it is useful to know the various categories into which fish fall. Firstly there are freshwater and salt-water fish (although salmon, eel and sea trout spend part of their lives in both). Then they are further categorised by their shape, round like a trout or flat like plaice. Most freshwater fish are round, all the flat fish are from the sea. This distinction is important in cooking in that a round fish will produce two fillets, slightly thicker in general, a flat fish four slender fillets.

Fish are also either oily – herring and salmon – or white-fleshed and non-oily, like sole and halibut; look out, too, for soft-textured fish which include several of the flat fish and some oily fish, or firm-textured (most round white fish). Most fish are fairly bony, perhaps one of the reasons why some people avoid eating fish, but a few are cartilaginous, their skeletons formed of white cartilage rather than bone (skate and monkfish, for example).

Shellfish

A simple collective term for a vast variety of fascinating and delectable marine creatures. They fall into two principal sub-divisions. *Crustaceans* are those with legs and a hard external skeleton (lobsters, shrimps, prawns, crabs and freshwater crayfish). *Molluscs* usually have a single or double shell, and can be further sub-divided into gastropods (whelks and winkles), bivalves (oysters, mussels, scallops and clams), and cephalopods which have a large head with tentacles (octopus, squid and cuttlefish).

Nutritional Value

One of the reasons fish plays such a major part in my Cuisine Naturelle cookery is that it contains so little fat; even the oil of oily fish is valuable in that it supplies vitamin D (present in little else, apart from sunlight), as well as fatty acids which are thought to be useful in protecting us from heart disease. Fish consists of high quality protein which is light and easily digested; it contains many vitamins and minerals as well.

Buying Fish and Shellfish

If you cannot catch them yourself and cook them the same day – when they are at their absolute best – you will need to rely on a good wet fish or specialist shop or market, and the advice of the experts there. In general, though, fresh whole fish should look wet and slippery, with a vibrant colour, taut skin, and silvery adhering scales; the gills should be sticky, moist, and deep red or maroon in colour; the eyes should be clear, protruding and slightly transparent. Fish pieces, steaks or fillets should have firm translucent flesh, white or pink according to variety, with an attractive sheen. All fresh fish should smell pleasant, with a tang of iodine, never sour or unpleasantly fishy.

Take your fish home and scale, clean and gut before immediately placing in the refrigerator, preferably on a plastic bag of ice, and covered. All fish bought from the fishmonger should be cooked on the day bought with the possible exception of sole and skate which, freshly caught, benefit from a day or two in the refrigerator.

Most of the shellfish used in this book should be alive – the mussels and scallops, for instance. They should be firmly closed, shells unbroken. Cephalopods should shimmer on the slab.

Don't be surprised at how much wastage there is on most fish and shellfish – it can be as high as 70 per cent on monkfish (its large head and heavy bones), and 60 per cent on unpeeled shrimps. Always work out your quantities carefully in advance, or ask the fishmonger's advice. If he or she is preparing the seafood for you, take the trimmings, skins, bones etc with you – those from white fish will make wonderful stock to use as the basis for a soup or sauce (see page 195).

Scaling Fish

It is best to do this first, but you may need to cut off spines and fins – of sea bass, for instance. Hold the fish by the tail in a cloth, and, using the blunt back of a knife, scrape away from you, against the direction of the scales. Do this under running water, or as close as possible to a good supply of water, as the scales tend to stick to all surfaces when dry.

Gutting Fish

To gut a round fish, see the Tips on pages 105 and 138. *To gut a flat fish*, remove the head with two diagonal cuts towards the pectoral fins. The intestines will come away with the head. Rinse and pat dry.

Skinning Fish

See the Tip on page 96.

Filleting Fish

To fillet a round fish, lay it on a board, tail towards you. Remove the head and cut along the length of the backbone from head to tail, cutting deep enough to expose the backbone (1). Insert the knife between fillet and ribs, and cut down the length of the fillet, using short diagonal strokes to separate fillet from backbone and ribs (2). Cut away completely. Hold the fish by its backbone, and separate lower fillet from ribs (3). Cut off at tail and head. Pull out any remaining tiny bones with tweezers.

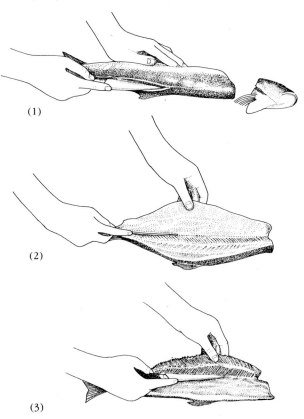

(1)

(2)

(3)

To fillet a flat fish, cut off the head and fins and cut along length of backbone (1). Slide a flexible knife under one fillet and, resting it on the backbone, cut until fillet is freed, using short movements (2). Remove and repeat with remaining three fillets.

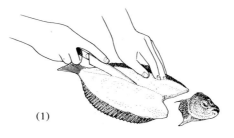

(1)

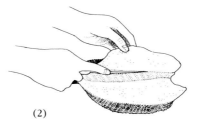

(2)

Cooking Fish and Shellfish

Basically, fish and shellfish should be cooked as briefly as possible, otherwise the flesh dries out, losing its juices and, most importantly, its taste. Moreover, it can also toughen and disintegrate. Neither should fish be cooked at too high a temperature. The recipes in this chapter and others throughout the book will advise as to suitable timings and temperature which will give you a 'feel' for cooking fish in general. And 'feel' is very important in cooking fish, for you need to feel the texture of the fish with your fingers to tell if it is cooked. It's one of my basic instructions to my young chefs, and this culinary touch can be learned in time (see the Tip on page 137).

I like to cook fish on the bone as much as possible as, like meat, a lot of the flavour is concentrated there. And again like meat, do season the fish well *before* cooking, because once the texture of the flesh is firmed by cooking, seasoning cannot penetrate.

Grilling or Barbecuing

Both are healthy methods of cooking whole fish, especially oilier ones, and for medium-sized fillets or portions. Never overheat the grill, and baste constantly with a marinade or oil to prevent the fish becoming too dry. I often leave skin on whole fish or fish fillets to be grilled as the fat underneath bastes the fish and keeps it moist. The skin is delicious, too, when crisp and brown! When grilling or barbecuing whole fish, it is often advisable to make a few diagonal cuts in the sides: this allows the heat to penetrate and cook the fish more evenly. Gently rub oil, seasoning and aromatics into these cuts for a superb result.

Poaching

This is a traditional method of cooking fish; it is gentle and helps retain the flavour and delicate texture of whole fish or pieces. The liquid – be it court bouillon, fish stock or milk – must not bubble, as any higher temperature will mean moisture from the fish is lost into the liquid.

Steaming

One of my favourite methods of cooking small fish or pieces as it is so gentle. If you like to cook fish often, investing in a proper steamer is well worth while. Spread the bottom of the perforated pan or basket insert with perforated foil and place the fish on in a single layer. The liquid beneath can be water, but I always prefer to add flavourings, or make up a court bouillon in advance (see page 196). Flavourings or a marinade can be added to the fish as well, in which case steam on a plate. The lid must be tight-fitting.

Sautéing

Use a good oil like groundnut or olive for the best colour and flavour, or clarified butter (see page 36), which does not burn. Dry fish well first, and drain well afterwards on kitchen paper.

Baking

An easy way of cooking whole fish, large or small, as well as fish steaks. Baste with a little wine, butter or marinade, or sauce if relevant.

Marinating

Many fish can be eaten *without* cooking. I have included several recipes for fish which is 'cooked' simply by being marinated in an acidic marinade, usually lime juice. Fish to be served thus – salmon, turbot, scallops etc – must be absolutely fresh. (Other fish which can be eaten uncooked are smoked fish and salted preserved fish such as *matjes* herrings.)

SEAFOOD RENDEZVOUS

This dish, which can be both first or main course, should be made using whatever fish or shellfish is fresh and in season. Simply keep to the proportions given.

Serves 4

8 freshwater crayfish, cooked	Shell, but keep the heads of four to garnish.
4 large scallops with coral	Open with the tip of a strong knife. Remove scallops and coral and wash quickly (do not leave in water). Pat dry.
100 g (4 oz) each of red snapper, salmon, turbot and John Dory fillets, skinned	Cut each variety of fish into four pieces.
salt and freshly ground pepper	Season all the seafood.
4 raw banana prawns, or cooked prawns, in the shell	Prepare by shelling.
30 g (1¼ oz) mixed leek, carrot and celeriac, trimmed and cut into very thin strips **20 ml** (4 tsp) olive oil	Sweat the vegetables in the olive oil in a wide, shallow pan, about 1 minute. Add the red snapper and sauté for about 30 seconds on each side. Add the turbot, John Dory and raw banana prawns, and sauté for 1 minute. Add the scallops and salmon at the very last moment, for seconds only.
25 ml (1 fl oz) Noilly Prat **50 ml** (2 fl oz) dry white wine **200 ml** (7 fl oz) fish stock (see page 195)	Add, and bring to the boil. Remove the seafood and vegetables with a perforated spoon, and keep warm. Strain the stock into a clean pan and reduce by boiling to almost nothing.
1 quantity white wine sauce (see page 199)	Add, and reduce slightly to the required consistency – a thin cream. Return the seafood and vegetables to the sauce. Carefully move around in the sauce, keeping pieces intact.
cayenne pepper	Taste for seasoning, and add some cayenne and a little more Noilly Prat and fish stock if the sauce is not thin enough. Finally add the crayfish (and cooked prawns if used) to warm through.
12 basil leaves	Shred the basil and add to the dish, then serve. Garnish each plate with a crayfish head.

TIP

Skinning fish It is generally better to skin fish, round or flat, once filleted. To do this, place the fillet skin side down and, using a *sharp* knife and short diagonal strokes, separate the fillet from the skin. The one exception to this rule is sole, which should be skinned before filleting. To skin sole, cut through the skin above the tail. Pull the skin up and back towards the head (a little salt on your fingers will ensure a good grip).

Skinning a fish fillet

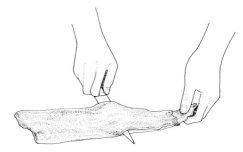

Skinning sole

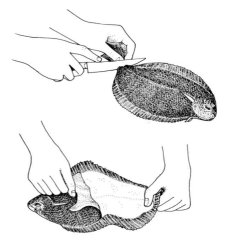

A SOUP OF JOHN DORY AND MUSSELS

A more substantial soup, using the firm flesh of the St Pierre or John Dory as well as mussels. It has a wonderful flavour.

Serves 4

approx **350 g** (12 oz) John Dory, filleted and skinned, all trimmings reserved

Cut the fillets at an angle into eight very thin slices. Cover and leave in the refrigerator.

16 mussels, thoroughly cleaned (see below) 225 ml (8 fl oz) dry white wine	Cook mussels very gently in half the wine in a shallow pan just until the shells open. Remove from the shells and keep the mussels to one side in their juices. Discard any that are still closed.
20 g (¾ oz) unsalted butter	Cook the skin and bones from the fish in one-third of the butter for 2–3 minutes in a deep pan.
a piece of leek, shallot and thyme from ingredients below	Add 425 ml (¾ pint) water and the flavourings, and simmer for 10–15 minutes. Strain into a jug and reserve.
25 g (1 oz) shallots, finely chopped	Cook in the remaining butter for 2–3 minutes.
25 g (1 oz) white part of leek, cut into fine strips a few threads of saffron 1 clove garlic, crushed	Add, and cook for 4–5 minutes.
50 g (2 oz) tomatoes, seeded and cut into fine strips	Add with the remaining wine and leave to reduce over a low heat for 2 minutes.
300 ml (½ pint) reduced fish stock (see page 195)	Add 300 ml (½ pint) of the John Dory stock, the fish stock, and mussel juice, strained through a fine cloth.
salt and freshly ground pepper	Add seasoning to taste, and skim if necessary. Just before serving, bring the soup up to the boil then remove from the heat.
a few leaves of fresh thyme 16 baby carrots or small slices of carrot, very lightly cooked 16 small slices of courgette, very lightly cooked 15 g (½ oz) lentil sprouts	Add herb, vegetables, sprouts, fish and mussels. Serve immediately in warm bowls.

TIP
To clean mussels, pull the beards off – the threads attached to the hinge – and scrub the shells clean, scraping off any barnacles with a strong knife. Place in clean water with a little salt for a couple of hours to help cleanse of sand. Throw away any that are broken, or that remain open when tapped sharply.

MUSSEL SOUP WITH SAFFRON

I love mussels, and think they are not used enough in Great Britain. They are fairly inexpensive, and are very versatile – you could use them in soups as here, in the famous *moules marinière* recipe (see page 101), with pasta, on pizzas, with saffron, white wine or curry sauces, and they can also be baked.

Serves 4

1 kg (2¼ lb) mussels	Scrape and clean thoroughly (see page 97).
75 g (3 oz) mixed onion, celeriac, carrot and leek, very finely diced **20 g** (¾ oz) butter	Sweat about one-third of the vegetables in half the butter in a suitable pot. Do not allow to brown.
a few sprigs of parsley and thyme **100 ml** (4 fl oz) dry white wine **600 ml** (a good pint) fish stock (see page 195)	Add the mussels with the herbs, white wine and 100 ml (4 fl oz) of the fish stock. Bring to the boil, cover, and simmer for 3–4 minutes, until the mussels are all open. Take the mussels out of the pan and out of their shells, discarding any that are still closed. Strain the cooking liquor through a muslin cloth and retain. Sweat the remaining vegetable dice in the remaining butter in the same pan for about 2 minutes.
a few threads of saffron	Add, and sweat for a few minutes, mixing well. Add the mussel liquor and remaining fish stock. Boil to reduce slightly.
100 ml (4 fl oz) double cream	Add, and bring to the boil again. Strain the soup into another pan, reserving the vegetable dice. Put half the mussels – keep the nice ones – back into the soup, and liquidise. Pour into a clean pan.
salt and freshly ground pepper	Put the soup back on to the heat, add the vegetable dice, and correct seasoning.
a little plucked chervil	Serve the soup in soup plates or bowls and garnish with the remaining mussels and the chervil.

TIP
Although threads of pure saffron are so expensive, they are worth it in terms of colour and flavour. Many of the saffron powders are not 100 per cent pure. Turmeric could be used instead, but the flavour will not be the same.

MOULES MARINIÈRE

Immediately you cross the Channel, you will see great bowls of steaming mussels on the tables of quayside cafés and respectable restaurants alike. Mussels are highly nutritious, containing calcium, iodine and iron. They also contain few calories, a fact much appreciated by seafood lovers! The butter adds a sweet smoothness to the sauce, but can be omitted if preferred.

Serves 4

1.5 kg (3½ lb) small to medium mussels	Wash and scrub well (see page 97). Place in a large shallow pan, in one layer if possible.
300 ml (½ pint) fish stock (see page 195) **100 ml** (4 fl oz) dry white wine **40 g** (1½ oz) shallots, finely chopped	Add, and cover. Simmer until the mussels open, about 3–4 minutes. Discard any that are still closed. Strain the cooking liquor immediately through muslin into a clean saucepan. Boil to reduce by one-third. Keep the mussels warm.
100 g (4 oz) unsalted butter, cut in small cubes salt and freshly ground pepper	Stir butter in, piece by piece, off the heat, and adjust seasoning.
15 ml (1 tbsp) lemon juice **15 ml** (1 tbsp) mixed chopped herbs (parsley, thyme and dill)	Add, and stir in well. Remove the top shell of each mussel if you wish. Arrange the mussels in an open dish, and pour the sauce over.
a few sprigs of parsley, chopped	Sprinkle over the mussels, and serve immediately.

FISH CAKES

These are comforting food, normally made using leftover mashed potato and fish. Here I have given two alternatives, raising the profile of the humble fish cake slightly! Serve for dinner, a lunch, or even for breakfast.

Makes 8

250 g (9 oz) potatoes, peeled	Cook in salted water until tender. Drain and stir in a hot pan over heat to dry out. Sieve them into a bowl.
350 g (12 oz) fish fillets (salmon, turbot, or other) salt and freshly ground pepper 100 ml (4 fl oz) fish stock (see page 195) 10 ml (2 tsp) dry white wine	Season and poach the fish in the fish stock and wine for about 2 minutes until just opaque in the thickest part. Drain, then cool slightly. Skin and flake into largish pieces.
30 ml (2 tbsp) chopped parsley 15 ml (1 tbsp) finely cut basil 1 large egg yolk, beaten	Add the fish to the potato and season. Add the herbs, and bind with the egg yolk.
plain flour for dusting	Turn the mixture on to a lightly floured board, and form into a thick roll. Divide and cut into eight slices. Shape into neat fish cakes and place in the refrigerator to firm up slightly.
2 eggs, beaten 150 g (5 oz) fresh white breadcrumbs 15 ml (1 tbsp) oil 50 g (2 oz) butter	Coat the fish cakes with beaten egg and breadcrumbs, then shallow-fry gently in the oil and butter until crisp and golden brown in colour.
1 quantity tomato or parsley sauce (see pages 198 and 199) 2 lemons	Drain well, and serve with parsley or tomato sauce, and lemon to squeeze over.

Variation

Use approximately the same quantities of potato, fish and herbs as in the previous recipe. Oil a frying pan and arrange as many large round metal crumpet or pikelet rings in the pan as it will hold.

Peel and grate the potatoes, and squeeze lightly to rid them of excess moisture. Place a thin layer of raw potato inside the rings, and cook. When the bottoms have firmed up and the potato is cooked, add a piece of fish of your choice to fit the inside of the rings. Sprinkle with some chopped mixed herbs and season with salt and pepper. Cover with another layer of grated potato and press in place. Turn the rings over carefully with a palette knife and press down. Finish cooking the second side. Drain well, and serve as above with tomato or parsley sauce.

BAKED SARDINES

There is nothing nicer than fresh sardines for an informal meal, and this simple sauce complements them well. Cool the sardines for a while after cooking, as they should be served warm, not hot. Serve with chilled red wine and a loaf of crusty bread.

Serves 4	**Oven**: moderate, 180°C/350°F/Gas 4
1 kg (2¼ lb) fresh sardines	Scale by rubbing carefully, then gut, and remove the heads.
salt and freshly ground pepper **15 ml** (1 tbsp) olive oil	Season fish, and brush with half the oil.
150 g (5 oz) tomatoes, skinned, seeded and diced (see page 124) **1** clove garlic, finely chopped **50 g** (2 oz) onions, finely chopped **40 g** (1½ oz) parsley, finely chopped **20 g** (¾ oz) dill, finely cut **100 ml** (4 fl oz) dry white wine	Mix together, and season to taste. Brush a shallow ovenproof dish with oil, and add the tomato mixture. Place the sardines on top, pushing them down into the mixture. Sprinkle with any remaining oil. Cook in the preheated oven for 5–6 minutes only.

YOUNG SALTED HERRING WITH WARM POTATOES

Matjes herrings, properly speaking, are the new season's young fish that have not yet reached maturity. They are caught and salted each spring, and are quite delicious. For an extra dimension, you could serve some soured cream mixed with finely snipped chives with the warm potatoes.

Serves 4

8 *matjes* fillets	Cut into pieces.
300 ml (½ pint) milk	Soak fish for 30 minutes in the milk, then drain well, and dry on kitchen paper.
100 g (4 oz) lean bacon, cut into strips	Warm through in a non-stick pan.
100 g (4 oz) onions, finely chopped	Add, and sauté. Do not allow to colour.
15 ml (1 tbsp) finely chopped parsley	Stir in.
freshly ground black pepper	Arrange the herring pieces on individual plates, season, and pour the warm onion and bacon mixture on top.
400 g (14 oz) small potatoes, freshly cooked in their skins	Serve, still warm, with the herring.

TIP
To bone fresh herrings, cut off the heads, but leave the tails on. Cut along the belly, gut and open out on a board, skin side up. Press flat along the backbone to loosen it. Turn over and prise out the backbone and side bones, starting at the head. Use tweezers to pick out any side bones missed.

TIP
To gut round fish through the belly, cut from the gills to the rear vent and pull out the intestines: do this with tweezers for sardines, with a spoon for a large fish such as a salmon. Carefully remove any traces of blood, rinse well and pat dry.

SALMON RILLETTES

This makes a delicious and unusual starter. Serve on toasted French or farmhouse bread.

Serves 4

200 g (7 oz) fillet of fresh salmon, skinned and boned	Trim and cut into very small dice.
15–30 ml (1–2 tbsp) lime juice	Sprinkle half over the salmon. Put to one side.
150 g (5 oz) smoked salmon, in a piece	Dice and sprinkle with juice as above.
80–100 g (3–4 oz) smoked cod's roe	Remove the skin and place in a large bowl. Crush with a fork.
30 ml (2 tbsp) double cream, or fromage frais **30 g** (1¼ oz) finely cut dill **5 ml** (1 tsp) very finely chopped green pepper **5 ml** (1 tsp) brandy	Add to the bowl, and mix well. Mix the fresh salmon and smoked salmon into the cod's roe mixture.
salt and freshly ground pepper	Season to taste, and spoon into a suitable dish or individual ramekins. Leave in a cool place for a minimum of 2 hours.

TIP
For a change in flavour, try a good Russian vodka or Kümmel instead of the brandy, and chives instead of the dill.

MARINATED SALMON AND HALIBUT

Fish prepared this way is eaten virtually raw, only 'cooked' by the action of the lime juice – something I learned about when I lived in Japan. Any firm white-fleshed fish can be marinated similarly – turbot, sea bass, tuna or scallops. The fish must be extremely fresh.

Serves 4

250 g (9 oz) fillet of Scottish salmon **200 g** (7 oz) fillet of halibut	Skin and carefully bone. Remove dark spot from the salmon (this is the fat). Cut fish into fine strips and arrange equal amounts of both on four plates.

1 lime, juiced
5 ml (1 tsp) coriander
  seeds, lightly crushed
salt and freshly ground
  white pepper
	Sprinkle over the fish, then season.

50 ml (2 fl oz) good olive oil	Spoon equal amounts over the fish.
a few chervil leaves, plucked	Add, and allow to stand for 3–4 minutes. The colour of the fish will change as it 'cooks' in the marinade. Serve immediately with warm plain toast or garlic bread.

TIP

To get as much juice as possible out of any citrus fruit, before cutting roll it a couple of times under your hand on a firm surface.

MONKFISH TERIYAKI WITH DAIKON NOODLES AND BABY LEEKS

Monkfish is another fish, like skate, that is ideal for those people who are frightened of fish bones – there is only one central bone, the rest being meat. The steaks can be simply grilled, with little or no oil, or turned into a *teriyaki* as here. You could also 'grill' the steaks in an oven with heat from above – simply turn them more often.

1 daikon radish, peeled	Using a mandoline cutter, finely slice lengthwise. Stack a few lengths at a time on top of each other, and cut finely into noodle-like strips with a large knife. Soak in iced water for about 30 minutes.
4 monkfish steaks with bones, about 250 g (9 oz) each salt and freshly ground pepper	Lightly season the fish and allow to stand for 15 minutes to firm up slightly.
150 ml (¼ pint) *mirin* **100 ml** (4 fl oz) *sake* **75 ml** (3 fl oz) dark soy sauce	Mix the *teriyaki* sauce ingredients together and marinate the steaks in it for 1 hour. Pat dry just before cooking.
olive oil	Either grill or pan-fry in a little oil in a skillet under or over a medium-high heat at first. Reduce the heat, and when the first side is golden brown, about 4–5 minutes, turn. When the fish is half done coat well with half the sauce. Finish cooking the second side (about another 4–5 minutes), occasionally brushing on more sauce.
about **9** baby leeks, trimmed and cut into 5 cm (2 in) lengths	Meanwhile, lightly brush the leeks with oil, and grill or pan-fry until golden brown. Serve the steaks garnished with the well drained cold daikon noodles and the warm baby leeks.

ROULADE OF MONKFISH WITH SALMON MOUSSE

A slightly more complicated recipe using monkfish, but a wonderful dish to serve for a special dinner party.

Serves 4

Oven: moderate, 180°C/350°F/Gas 4

150 g (5 oz) salmon fillet, finely cut salt **1 egg white**	Make the salmon mousse first. Purée the salmon in the processor with a little salt, then add the egg white and process until smooth.
150 ml (¼ pint) double cream, icy cold **15 ml** (1 tbsp) Noilly Prat	Remove the purée to a chilled bowl over ice, and beat in the cream and Noilly Prat, a little at a time, with a wooden spoon. (The mousse must not get too warm, or it might split.)
freshly ground pepper **30 g** (1¼ oz) mixed carrot, leek and green beans, trimmed, finely diced, and blanched	Correct seasoning and fold in the vegetables.
4 monkfish steaks, about 150 g (5 oz) each	Trim and remove the centre bones carefully from each. Fill the space left by the bones with the mousse, and spread a thin layer of mousse over the steaks, to cover them, as well.
20 large spinach leaves, trimmed and blanched	Wrap the outside edges of the steaks in the spinach and season.
50 g (2 oz) butter, melted	Arrange steaks on a buttered baking dish. Brush with melted butter and bake in the preheated oven for 15–20 minutes.
1 quantity white wine sauce (see page 199)	Serve with the white wine sauce.

MONKFISH STRIPED WITH CARROT AND CORIANDER

This dish looks magnificent with its overlapping stripes of red and green.

Serves 4

Oven: moderately hot, 190°C/375°F/Gas 5

1 monkfish tail, about 1 kg (2¼ lb) **50 ml** (2 fl oz) olive oil salt and freshly ground pepper **15 ml** (1 tbsp) cut herbs (chives, basil, parsley)	Trim the fish well, and brush lightly with some of the oil. Season and sprinkle with cut herbs.
1 large carrot, trimmed 1 large courgette, trimmed	Finely slice lengthwise with a mandoline cutter, then blanch separately in boiling salted water. Refresh and dry on a cloth or kitchen paper. Wrap the fish alternately with the long carrot and courgette 'scales', overlapping them across the width.
1 piece caul fat, about 30 × 60 cm (12 × 24 in)	Place the sheet of caul fat on the tail, fold over and under and wrap neatly. Trim off any spare bits. Tie with string.
25 g (1 oz) butter, melted	Spread over a suitable dish with the remaining oil, add the fish, and bake in the preheated oven for about 20 minutes, basting frequently.
1 quantity tomato sauce (see page 198) 2 lemons, halved	Serve with the tomato sauce and lemon.

TIP

Caul is a strong, virtually transparent membrane, set with particles of fat, that surrounds the paunch of mammals. That used in cookery is from the pig, and you should be able to order it from a good butcher. *Crépine* in French, it is used as a covering for the small sausages called *crépinettes*, and the Provençal version called *gayettes*. In English cookery, it was called 'flead', and was used, again as a covering, in the making of haslet and faggots. A familiar usage is as the wrapping of the Greek sausages, *sheftalia*, and here it is used to keep the garnish 'stripes' in place, the caul basting the fish while it is cooked. Soak dry-salted caul in warm water to soften before using; with fresh this is not necessary. (If you can't get any caul, carefully wrap the fish in foil.)

MONKFISH WITH MIXED PEPPERS AND HERBS

The pepper and herb mixture can be prepared in advance and kept in the refrigerator.

Serves 4

550 g (1¼ lb) monkfish fillet, trimmed	Slice into twelve even pieces.
25 ml (1 fl oz) olive oil **25 g** (1 oz) onion, finely sliced ½ clove garlic, crushed	Heat the oil and cook the onion and garlic slowly for 2–3 minutes.
50 g (2 oz) each of red, green and yellow peppers, seeded, trimmed and sliced **2.5 ml** (½ tsp) chopped tarragon **2.5 ml** (½ tsp) each of chopped parsley and finely cut chives	Add, and cook slowly for a further 2–3 minutes.
100 g (4 oz) butter	In a large lidded frying pan, seal the fish in a little of the butter, but do not allow to colour. Add the prepared pepper mixture. Cut the remainder of the butter into cubes and chill.
100 ml (4 fl oz) dry vermouth **300 ml** (½ pint) fish stock (see page 195)	Pour over the fish. Cover and poach for about 5 minutes. Remove the fish and peppers with a slotted spoon and keep warm. Reduce the liquor to about 200 ml (7 fl oz) in a small pan. Add the cubes of butter gradually to the sauce on a low heat, shaking the pan gently to swirl in each cube before adding the next.
approx **2.5 ml** (½ tsp) lemon juice	Check the seasoning, adding a little lemon juice if necessary. Return the fish and peppers to the pan and warm gently without boiling. Place the fish on warmed plates, add the peppers and pour the sauce around.

SEA BASS ON MULTICOLOURED NOODLES

Fish goes well with pasta, and if you use three different colours of noodles, this dish looks very good.

Serves 4

600 g (1 lb 5 oz) fillet of bass, with skin salt and freshly ground pepper	Cut into four portions. Pat dry, and season.
40 g (1½ oz) butter **1** shallot, finely chopped	Butter a suitable heatproof dish with half the butter and add the shallot. Place the bass fillets on top.
50 ml (2 fl oz) dry white wine **100 ml** (4 fl oz) fish stock (see page 195)	Add, and cover. Bring quickly to the boil, on top of the stove, and then simmer gently for 2–3 minutes. Remove the fillets and keep warm. Reduce the cooking liquor by half by rapid boiling.
150 ml (¼ pint) double cream	Add, and continue to boil until the sauce coats the back of a spoon.
5 ml (1 tsp) finely chopped tarragon	Add, and adjust the seasoning.
100 g (4 oz) each of tomato, spinach and saffron egg noodles (see page 203)	Cook in plenty of boiling, salted water. Rinse and drain. Toss in the remaining butter over a moderate heat, then arrange on four heated serving plates. Carefully cut each bass fillet in half. Arrange on top of the noodles. Pour over the tarragon sauce.

RED SNAPPER WITH TOMATO VINAIGRETTE

I am a great believer in simplicity, and this recipe is just that, very simple and very good. The fish should be served lukewarm, not hot. If you like you could warm the carrot slices through in the steamer along with the fish – or you could use samphire as an accompaniment. This is a wonderful vegetable for fish, in season in Britain in May, and imported from April to July. Buy it at fishmongers.

Serves 4

4 fillets red snapper, about 150 g (5 oz) each salt and freshly ground pepper	Season and place in a steamer.
1 sprig dill	Place on top of the fish.
2 medium tomatoes, seeded and diced (see page 124) 50 ml (2 fl oz) red wine vinegar 100 ml (4 fl oz) olive oil 20 g (¾ oz) shallot, finely chopped 15 ml (1 tbsp) finely cut chives	To make the tomato vinaigrette, mix all the ingredients together, and season to taste. Warm very gently.
court bouillon (see page 196)	Steam the fillets over boiling court bouillon for about 2–3 minutes. The fillets should curl a bit, which is a sign of freshness. Arrange the fish on a plate or dish with the skin uppermost, and cover with the tomato vinaigrette.
25 g (1 oz) carrot, peeled, scored, finely sliced and blanched 15 g (½ oz) tiny turned chunks of courgette, blanched 4 sprigs chervil	Use to garnish the fish.

TIP

To score or *canneler* a vegetable, you need a special knife – often described as a citrus or mushroom scorer, and available in good kitchen shops. These have a tiny single-pronged cutting edge (on the side or top) which, when drawn along mushroom cap, lemon peel or peeled carrot side, produces a groove and a long strip of the vegetable or peel. If you do this at regular intervals around the carrot or lemon, a slice when cut will have attractive serrated edges.

SEA BREAM WITH GARLIC

A whole fish can very easily be sautéed as here, in some good olive oil with a flavour of garlic (you could use *more* garlic if you wanted, of course, or use a garlic-flavoured oil).

Serves 4

1 sea bream, about 1 kg (2¼ lb), scaled and cleaned salt and freshly ground pepper	Wash and dry the fish well, and season.
2 cloves garlic, unpeeled, crushed 15 ml (1 tbsp) each of water and milk, mixed	Soak the garlic in the liquid for a few minutes to soften its pungency. Drain and dry.
100 ml (4 fl oz) olive oil	Heat in a suitable pan until almost smoking hot. Add the fish and the garlic and sauté the fish on each side for about 5–6 minutes. Baste constantly with a spoon. Remove the fish from the pan, drain well, and place on a hot serving plate. Pour off the oil from the pan.
60 g (2¼ oz) butter 60 ml (4 tbsp) finely chopped parsley	Add to the pan, and heat until sizzling.
½ lemon, juiced	Add to the hot butter, then pour over the fish and serve.

BAKED RED SEA BREAM

There are many varieties of bream, but the red and black are the only members of the family which come as far as northern Europe. The red is one of those considered to be best, with lean, firm, white meat.

Serves 4

Oven: moderately hot, 190°C/375°F/Gas 5

1 red sea bream, about 1 kg (2¼ lb), scaled and cleaned salt and freshly ground pepper 15 g (½ oz) butter	Season the fish and place it in a buttered ovenproof dish.
3 tomatoes, sliced ½ small cucumber, sliced	Spread over the fish.

1 medium onion, finely
   chopped
1 bay leaf
20 g (¾ oz) parsley, finely
   chopped
1 green pepper, seeded and
   diced
15–30 ml (1–2 tbsp) lemon
   juice
30 ml (2 tbsp) olive oil

Mix the remaining ingredients together, season to taste, and sprinkle over the top of the fish.
Cover with buttered paper, place the dish in the preheated oven, and bake for about 30 minutes. Serve whole from the dish.

TURBOT FILLET IN CABBAGE LEAVES WITH PEPPER SAUCES

The pepper sauces, one yellow and one red, contrast beautifully with the green of the cabbage and the white of the fish.

Serves 4

4 turbot fillets, about 150 g
   (5 oz) each
salt and freshly ground
   pepper
4 Savoy cabbage (or
   lettuce) leaves, ribs
   removed, blanched and
   refreshed

Season fillets, and wrap half of each with a cabbage leaf. Set aside in the top half of a steamer.

2 large peppers, 1 yellow,
   1 red, seeded

Cut into large pieces.

30 ml (2 tbsp) olive oil
1 shallot, sliced
2 small cloves garlic,
   crushed with skin on

Heat oil in a suitable pan and sweat the shallot and garlic without browning.
Divide the shallot mixture between two saucepans, and add the yellow pepper pieces to one, the red to the other.

2 sprigs thyme
1 litre (1¾ pints) fish stock
   (see page 195)

Put a sprig of thyme and 175 ml (6 fl oz) of the fish stock in each pan, cover, bring to the boil, and simmer briskly for about 15 minutes until the pepper is tender. Stir occasionally.
Remove thyme and garlic from each pan, then liquidise the mixtures separately until smooth. Sieve if wished. Season to taste.
Steam the prepared fish over the remaining fish stock for about 3–4 minutes.
Arrange some of the two well seasoned hot sauces carefully on individual plates, and place the fish fillets on top.

M

POACHED SKATE WITH LEMON BUTTER

Skate is a fish that is underused, I think, but it is so simple to cook and eat, with no sharp bones. You could serve it with hollandaise or a similar butter sauce, or with a cold herb dressing, but I like it poached, then served with a simple lemon-flavoured butter.

Serves 4

1.25–1.4 kg (2¾–3 lb) skate wing (or 2 wings, each about 675 g/1½ lb), skinned	Cut into four pieces altogether, and put into a suitably wide pan.
2 litres (3½ pints) court bouillon (see page 196), containing a little white wine vinegar **50 g** (2 oz) carrots, peeled, scored and sliced (see page 117) freshly ground pepper a pinch of cayenne pepper	Cover fish with the unstrained boiling court bouillon, add the carrot, and season to taste. Put the pan on a low heat, cover and simmer (without boiling) for 8–10 minutes (20–25 if the fish pieces are larger). Drain the fish and place on a warm plate. Strain the court bouillon, and scatter the carrot slices over the fish.
25 g (1 oz) slightly salted butter salt 1 lemon, juiced	Melt butter, and season with salt, pepper and lemon juice. Pour over the fish.
15 ml (1 tbsp) flat parsley leaves	Sprinkle over, then serve immediately.

TIP
If you are using a whole or large piece of fish, put in the pan with *cold* court bouillon, then bring to the boil and poach. If the fish is smaller or in pieces, use *boiling* court bouillon.

121

SEAFOOD AND CHICKEN WITH SAFFRON RICE

The rice for this dish must be fluffy, moist and succulent: not too dry and not too wet. It has many variations according to what is fresh and best in the market. You could add squid instead of octopus, for instance, and small sweet clams instead of or as well as mussels. Artichoke hearts, mushrooms and small pieces of sausage could be included too. The secret is to add all ingredients one at a time in the correct sequence so that, eventually, they will be cooked at the same moment.

Serves 4

225 g (8 oz) mussels, cleaned·(see page 97) **400 ml** (14 fl oz) fish stock (see page 195), simmering	Cook mussels in a little of the stock until open, as on page 101. Discard any that are still closed. Strain the juices through a cloth back into main pan of stock. Keep the mussels in the half shell, covered and moist.
100 g (4 oz) sole fillet, skinned and sliced salt and freshly ground pepper	Season, poach in a little of the stock for about 3 minutes, then strain the stock and return to the main pan. Keep the fish moist.
10 prawns or scampi, preferably raw **50 g** (2 oz) shrimps	If cooked, remove legs and trimmings, and simmer these in the stock to enrich it. If raw, simmer in stock for about 5–6 minutes, shell and reserve. Keep the heads on four prawns as a garnish.
50 ml (2 fl oz) olive oil **2** cloves garlic, skin on, lightly crushed	Heat the oil in a wide, very shallow pan. Sauté the garlic in it for a few minutes, then remove.
300 g (11 oz) chicken meat, mainly from legs and thighs, skinned and diced **100 g** (4 oz) lean pork, diced	Brown on all sides in the garlic-flavoured oil, stirring continuously.
75 g (3 oz) baby octopus or squid, cleaned and cut into small pieces	Add, and brown similarly, stirring continuously.

50 g (2 oz) peas, shelled
1 large onion, finely
    chopped
200 g (7 oz) mixed red,
    green and yellow
    peppers, seeded,
    trimmed and diced
2 large sweet tomatoes,
    seeded and sliced
	Add, in sequence, and stir until softened.

200 g (7 oz) long-grain rice	Add, and stir over a high heat until it becomes translucent.
100 ml (4 fl oz) dry white wine	Pour into the pan along with the hot strained stock. Add the prawns or scampi and the shrimps.

cayenne pepper
a pinch of saffron threads,
    infused in 15 ml (1 tbsp)
    water
	Season to taste, and add the saffron infusion.
	Stir once or twice with a spatula, and allow to simmer for about 5 minutes. Bring the seafood to the top to prevent it overcooking.
	Cover and simmer for about a further 10 minutes or until the rice is ready.
	Arrange the warm mussels, sole and other seafood over the top of the mixture in radiating patterns.

1–2 lemons, quartered **15 ml** (1 tbsp) freshly chopped parsley	Serve from the pan with lemon quarters and parsley.

TIP

To prepare squid, gently pull apart head and body. Cut tentacles above head, and discard the intestines, beak and ink sac (1). Remove transparent quill and membrane from inside body sac. Cut tentacles above head (2). Skin body pouch, and remove and skin fins (3). Rinse all well. Body, tentacles and fins are now ready for use.

To prepare octopus, cut off the tentacles, and then the top part of the body. The head, with the eyes, lies *between* body sac and tentacles and should be discarded. Turn the body sac inside out, and discard the intestines. Blanch in boiling water for 3–4 minutes and rub with salt to remove the skin. Cut the suckers off the tentacles and rinse all pieces well.

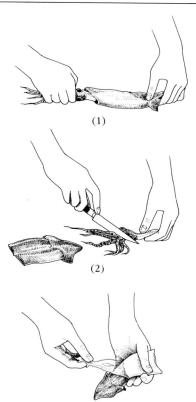

(1)

(2)

(3)

RED MULLET WITH CORIANDER AND TOMATO DRESSING

Another simple steamed fish recipe. If you like, you can leave the garlic skins on, crush lightly and add to the dressing, then remove just before serving. The flavour is less intense.

Serves 4

175 ml (6 fl oz) olive oil **5 ml** (1 tsp) lemon juice **2** cloves garlic, crushed **15 ml** (1 tbsp) coriander seeds, crushed	Whisk well together.
3 tomatoes, skinned (see below)	Cut into quarters, and scrape the seeds and juices into a small muslin-lined bowl. Gather up the muslin and squeeze tightly over the bowl to extract as much juice as possible. Discard seeds.
salt and freshly ground pepper	Add the dressing to the tomato juices then season to taste. Cut the remaining tomato flesh into the very tiniest dice possible and add to the dressing.
4 fillets red mullet, about 175 g (6 oz) each, carefully boned, with skin on	Steam the seasoned mullet for 3–4 minutes (see page 94).
8–10 small curly endive leaves	Place a small nest of endive leaves in the centre of each plate and season lightly with salt. Place the fish on top.
2.5 ml (½ tsp) each of finely cut chives, chopped parsley and thyme	Warm the dressing slightly, add herbs, and spoon carefully over the fish and salad.

TIP

To skin and dice tomatoes, remove their stalks and then blanch in boiling water for approximately 30 seconds. Plunge into iced water and peel. Cut the peeled tomatoes in half, remove and discard the seeds with a teaspoon, and then cut the flesh into tiny dice.

This is also the first stage in a very useful sauce, tomato concasse (see page 198).

PICNICS AND BARBECUES

I enjoyed fishing as a young boy, growing up amidst the beautiful Swiss countryside of lakes and meadows. I had a bicycle, and would travel for miles to find the right place to fish. With me I would take my mother's home-cooked bread, still warm from the oven, and would buy some Swiss cheese from the local dairy as I passed. This satisfied my hunger as I sat in my boat in the middle of the lake, waiting for the fish to bite. Later, in the cool of the early evening, I would light a small fire on the shore, very carefully as my father had taught me, and grill my fresh-caught fish. I always remembered to bring some salt, and a small bunch of rosemary to give fragrance . . .

I still love the freshness, the open-air feeling of eating outside. It's one of the great things of life, even if, in Great Britain, it's not possible to do it too often!

Eating outside involves simpler food – you're not juggling with intricate sauces and complicated timings – and this, I think, is one explanation of the truism that food always tastes better when eaten out of doors. With more basic foods, cooked in a simple way, you can taste the honesty and essence of the food itself.

Picnics

If barbecue eating is outdoor eating at home, picnics are generally thought of as outdoor eating *away* from home (although, of course, one can picnic quite legitimately in the garden or even inside if the weather dictates). Picnic foods, therefore, must be portable above all, and once again the simpler the better. Delicate decorated mousses are definitely not foods for the average picnic! However, most things *can* be transported happily with ingenuity: using clingfilm, rigid containers, cool bags and chill boxes. If foods are packaged firmly and correctly, they can survive a car journey and a trudge up or down dale, to riverbank or beach.

Picnic foods must be those which taste good cold or lukewarm (insulated boxes keep foods warm as well as cold). They must also be uncomplicated to eat. You can, of course, transport with you tables, chairs, a canteen of cutlery and your best glasses; I prefer a few rugs and cushions around an attractive cloth laid on the grass (but I do, I must admit, prefer real cutlery, plates and glasses to the disposable alternatives).

Pies, pastries, cakes and breads all transport well, as do potted meats, fish or game, bowls of pâté, cooked meat or poultry, and salads. If a salad requires dressing at the last minute, take the dressing in a screw-top jar. Separate little packages of seasoning and chopped herbs are always a good idea.

Picnic desserts can simply be fresh fruit: apples, pears, figs, apricots, peaches, nectarines, for example, can all be eaten easily. However, berries and cream can be taken in separate containers as well, as could fruit salads – plain or exotic as the occasion demands – or fruits in liqueur. Cheese is almost an essential.

Picnics have to be more organised than barbecues. You must remember to pack and take everything you will need, with no kitchen to rush into for that forgotten bottle opener. A bag for disposal of waste is a good addition to the picnic list, as is some water and cloths for wiping sticky hands. But never forget about the charms of an *impromptu* picnic, when you can take advantage of the 'fat of the land', so to speak. Whether you're in the wilds of Yorkshire or the Dordogne, you can buy some fresh bread, salad vegetables, salami, cheese, fruit and a bottle of local ale or wine, and truly enjoy a picnic meal to remember.

Barbecues

The first priority when planning a barbecue party (apart from anxiously monitoring the long-range weather forecast) is to select your guests and work out what foods they would appreciate. Most like meat, but for those who don't, you should think of fish, salads and other vegetable dishes. If there are children involved – and a barbecue is a feast that they enjoy particularly – their tastes must be taken into consideration too: however sophisticated they may appear to be, things like sausages, spare ribs, baked potatoes and garlic bread will never go wrong.

The second priority, inevitably, is a good barbecue. I have a brick-built one in my garden in Berkshire, plus one on wheels as back-up, given to me by American friends of the late Danny Kaye. Seek the advice of your friends as to the best to choose.

What I like best about barbecuing is that it is a form of grilling, one of the healthier methods of cooking. There is a certain amount of added fat – the oils and marinades basted on fish, fowl or flesh during the grilling – but most of this is burned away during the cooking. Because grilling flavours, the best possible cooking medium must be used, and a good charcoal is vital. Charcoal is generally available in two forms, as lumpwood or wood charcoal pieces, or as charcoal briquettes. The latter are probably better as they are made from hardwood (oak, beech and birch) which burns more evenly and more intensely for longer. (The Americans have a larger choice, and can use mesquite or hickory charcoal as well.) Firelighters, liquid or block, may be necessary, but as they can contaminate foods, must be burned off well before grilling starts.

Cooking must not start until the charcoal is an even white, when there are no black unburned parts of charcoal. Neither must there be any flames. Most people make the mistake of grilling far too early. Between lighting the barbecue and awaiting its readiness, there is a fairly relaxed time when you can have a drink and some conversation with your guests. Or this is when you could be finishing off the table, for I believe it should be as attractive as a table inside: with cloth, napkins, flowers, beautiful glasses and cutlery.

There never seems to be a lack of potential helpers for the cooking. My sons Philipp and Mark enjoy this, and usually there is a male guest or two who will quite happily don an apron and wield a pair of tongs. Someone must be there all the time, however, for when the foods go on the barbecue, they must be prevented from burning, they need to be turned at the right time (using tongs to avoid piercing the food and losing juices), and they should be basted to prevent them from becoming too dry. I use my own flavoured oils for this (see page 205). I also like to flavour the coals even more by burning pieces of onion on them, or bunches of herbs just as a food is ready to serve. A basting oil can be brushed on with a paintbrush, or often I use a bunch of herbs tied together. It is a good idea to use specially made grills, for fish and meat, which prevent the food from breaking up when turning.

Now for the food itself. Because a barbecue is inevitably close to the house, I like to prepare many things beforehand, and have a relaxed balance between charcoal-grilled foods and pre-prepared. It all depends on what you want to serve, how many you are serving, and indeed on how much cooking space there is on the barbecue. Potatoes, for instance, I would always choose to bake either in the oven (see page 44), or in a clay potato pot on the coals or top of the stove. A couple of starters could be pre-prepared in the kitchen, and these can be eaten, perhaps, while the charcoal is reaching its peak. The salads and desserts, too, will have been made in advance – although there are some vegetable and fruit dishes that can be happily cooked on the dying embers. Try my bananas in foil, or even a skewer of fruits marinated in a liqueur: a few moments over heat, and they are quite delectable.

I never see barbecues as a set meal, with one course following another in a logical progression; you eat whatever is ready and delicious, as it comes, which sometimes means eating a couple of courses together. A barbecue meal can be a long one but surrounded by friends and family on a perfect summer's afternoon, I can't think of anything I like better.

LEEK, YAM AND MOZZARELLA TART

Although the filo pastry is brittle, it can be taken on a picnic if you pack it carefully in a rigid box or tin. You could use other cheeses instead of the Mozzarella, such as Raclette or Edam, for instance. Make the pie in a 25 cm (10 in) tin with a removable base.

Serves 8

Oven: moderate, 160°C/325°F/Gas 3

450 g (1 lb) young leeks, well washed **1** small sprig thyme	Cut leeks into 1 cm (½ in) rings, then boil in water to cover, with the thyme, until soft, about 15 minutes. Drain well, reserving the liquor. Discard the thyme.
salt and freshly ground pepper **8** basil leaves, cut into fine strips	Season leeks with salt, pepper and basil.
225 g (8 oz) yam, peeled and cut into 6 mm (¼ in) slices	Cook in the leek liquor until just soft, about 7–8 minutes. Drain, and allow to cool.
200 g (7 oz) filo pastry, rolled out thinly (see page 202)	Divide into four 30 cm (12 in) squares. Place three pieces of pastry on top of each other in the tin and arrange alternate layers of yam and leek on top.
2 oz (50 g) butter, gently melted with a sprig of thyme (optional)	Trickle over the top.
175 g (6 oz) Mozzarella cheese, diced **1** cooking apple, peeled, cored, diced and tossed in lemon juice	Sprinkle over, and season. Top with the remaining sheet of filo and seal edges, using a little water. Prick several times with a fork and bake in the oven for about 20–30 minutes. If top starts to brown too quickly, reduce the heat or cover loosely with foil. Serve warm or cold.

TIP

There are several varieties of starchy tubers that are sold as yams. They are large, roughly cylindrical in shape, with a brown, rough skin, often with tiny hair rootlets attached. They are usually cut to a manageable size in West Indian and West African shops, and the flesh can be sticky yellow or white. Fairly bland in themselves, they add a potato-like texture to a pie such as the one above, and can be boiled, puréed, stewed and sautéed.

BROCCOLI, SPINACH AND SALMON TERRINE

This would be ideal for a Glyndebourne-type picnic – or as a starter for a barbecue 'picnic' in the garden.

Serves 10

900 g (2 lb) fresh fillet of salmon, with skin	The piece of fish must be approximately the length of a 1.5 litre (2½ pint) terrine.
salt and freshly ground pepper **1.5 litres** (2½ pints) fish stock or court bouillon (see pages 195 and 196)	Lightly season the fish and place in a pan with the chosen liquid.
1 sprig fresh dill (optional) ½ lemon, juiced (optional)	Add to the fish stock only, then lightly poach the salmon for 10–12 minutes. Leave to cool in the liquid over a bain-marie of ice. When cool, peel off skin and remove any brown parts. Strain and reserve the stock.
250 g (9 oz) broccoli, in small florets **2.5 litres** (4¼ pints) vegetable stock (see page 192)	Blanch broccoli in 1 litre (1¾ pints) of the vegetable stock then cool in the remaining cold vegetable stock over ice.
350 g (12 oz) spinach, thick stalks removed, washed	Blanch and cool as for broccoli. Place a layer of half the broccoli in the bottom of the terrine, then a layer of half the spinach. Place the fish on top, and cover with layers of the remaining spinach and broccoli.
6 leaves gelatine, soaked in cold water and squeezed dry	Dissolve in a quarter of the fish stock over a gentle heat. Make the volume up to 750 ml (1⅓ pints) with some of the remaining fish stock.
45 ml (3 tbsp) finely cut dill	Add 15 ml (1 tbsp) to the fish stock, and then chill until the consistency of raw egg white. Pour into the terrine carefully, and chill until set. Turn out carefully by dipping the terrine dish briefly in hot water, and cut in slices.
500 ml (18 fl oz) plain low-fat yoghurt **15 ml** (1 tbsp) English mustard	To make the sauce, mix together with the remaining cut dill. Add about 50 ml (2 fl oz) of the remaining fish stock if necessary.
dill sprigs	Serve each slice on individual plates on a little of the sauce, and garnish with a sprig of dill.

TIP
To make the turning out of the
terrine a little easier, line the dish
with clingfilm. Brush the dish
lightly with oil first which helps the
clingfilm to stick.

CERVELATS CORDON BLEU

Cervelats are Swiss sausages made from a mixture of veal or beef and pork, which are smoked to a golden brown. They have a good texture and are mild in flavour, which makes them popular with children. You don't have to use Cervelats, other sausages will do.

To cook on the barbecue, you don't need to egg and breadcrumb the sausages: simply cut a cross at each end of the cheese-stuffed sausage and grill over charcoal until cooked, when the cut ends will splay out decoratively.

Serves 4

4 Cervelat sausages	Cut in half lengthwise.
4 slices Emmental, Gruyère or similar English cheese	The slices should be the same shape as the half sausages. Put one slice on the lower half of each sausage, and replace the top with the cheese between. Fix each with two cocktail sticks.
2 eggs	Beat with a fork on a shallow wide plate and moisten the sausages all over.
250 g (9 oz) breadcrumbs	Roll the egged sausages in the crumbs until well covered.
600 ml (1 pint) vegetable oil	Deep-fry the coated sausages in hot oil until the crumbs are golden, about 5 minutes. Drain well and serve, with a green salad. They're also good with sweet pickled dill cucumbers and mustard, and shiny, polished red apples.

TIP
Fresh breadcrumbs can be large and ungainly, so allow slices of bread to dry out (in the warming drawer of the oven perhaps) before processing them to an even texture.

SPARE RIBS

I think there's nothing nicer than spare ribs which have been marinated overnight and then barbecued. There's not too much meat, but what there is is delicious – especially with my 'special' last-minute ingredient! Some chopped onion directly on the coals is a good idea too – the fragrance is quite delicious and permeates the ribs.

Serves 4

3–4 meaty Chinese-style pork ribs per person (see below)	Trim and, if in a rack, slice into separate ribs, always close against the right-hand bone.
2 cloves garlic 25 g (1 oz) fresh ginger root, peeled	Finely chop, then, using your hands, rub the mixture into the ribs.
30 ml (2 tbsp) each of hoisin sauce and yellow bean sauce 30 ml (2 tbsp) each of light and dark soy sauce 1 small orange, juiced 3 tomatoes, skinned and very finely chopped 2 sprigs basil, chopped 30 ml (2 tbsp) dry sherry or *sake* a pinch of sugar freshly ground black pepper	Place all the marinade ingredients in a saucepan and bring to the boil. Leave to cool, then pour over the ribs. Leave to marinate overnight. Grill the ribs over the barbecue for 15–25 minutes according to size, basting with the marinade and turning occasionally. (Or cook in the marinade in the oven, at 180°C/350°F/Gas 4 for about 45 minutes, turning halfway through.)
30 ml (2 tbsp) clear honey, warmed	About 5 minutes before the ribs are ready, brush with honey and finish the cooking.

TIP
The Chinese-style spare ribs to be marinated then roasted or charcoal-grilled, should not be confused with spare rib chops, which are cut from the meaty neck end. Spare ribs are cut from the thick end of the belly, and are usually bought in rack form. They can be marinated and grilled or roasted as a whole rack – easier to handle – but the flavours of the marinade and of the charcoal grilling permeate individual ribs much more effectively.

M

CLAY POT CHICKEN

This is a very simple, tasty recipe, and very healthy too because of the method of cooking – in a chicken brick. This has to be soaked in cold water for fifteen minutes while you prepare the vegetables. When heated, the clay releases steam which bastes the food in its own juices, making for moister, more aromatic cooking. There is no stuffing, except for the rosemary and garlic – a golden, flavourful corn-fed chicken should be as plain as possible and taste of . . . chicken.

Serves 4

Oven: moderately hot, 190°C/375°F/Gas 5

1 corn-fed chicken (about
    1.4 kg/3 lb in weight)
2 cloves garlic, crushed
    slightly, skin on
3 sprigs rosemary

Put the garlic and 1 rosemary sprig inside the chicken. Tie the chicken (see Tip).

salt and freshly ground
    pepper

Season the chicken well, rubbing it in with your hands.

2 medium carrots
2 small red onions
1 small leek
1 small swede
4 small parsnips

Trim, wash and peel as appropriate, and chop roughly. Arrange in the dampened clay pot, lightly season, and mix well.

2 sprigs thyme

Place the chicken on the bed of vegetables and add the remaining rosemary and the thyme.
Cover with the lid and bake in the preheated oven for about 1¼–1½ hours. Test to see that the juices run clear when the thickest part of the thigh is pierced with a thin skewer.
Carve the chicken, serve the vegetables, and spoon over the juices.

TIP
A chicken is tied to keep it in good shape. Take a long length of thin string and tie the legs of the bird together, knotting it well and leaving a cut length. I then like to break the ribs of a bird, which enables the breasts to plump out well: lay the chicken on its side and just press your weight down on the breast until you hear and feel a crack. To finish the tying process, pass the long end of the string up one side of the bird, and down the other, catching the wings. Tie firmly to the length of string left free earlier.

CHARCOAL-GRILLED SEA BASS WITH FENNEL

The herb fennel, and by association the bulb of Florence fennel, has long been eaten with fish, and indeed it is often called the 'fish herb'. All parts of the plant – leaves, stems and seeds – are aromatic and can be used in cookery. If you grow your own herb, you can dry the stems and use them as below with fish or shellfish, or with barbecued lamb, burning the dried stems on the actual coals, so that the aniseed-flavoured oils permeate the food.

Serves 8

1 large whole sea bass, approx 1.8–2.25 kg (4–5 lb)	Clean through the gills (see page 138). Rinse thoroughly until the water runs clear, then dry.
3 medium fennel bulbs	To prepare the stuffing, remove and keep the feathery tops of the bulbs. Cut bulbs in half lengthwise, remove and discard hard cores, and finely slice.
2 onions, finely sliced **100 ml** (4 fl oz) olive oil salt and freshly ground pepper	Sweat onion and fennel gently in 30 ml (2 tbsp) of the olive oil until just tender, and season with salt and pepper. Add the chopped fennel fronds and leave to cool. Spoon and pack stuffing into the fish through the mouth, or use a piping bag.
dried fennel stalks **1** lemon, zested in strips, and juiced	Place the fish on a suitable tray with the dried fennel stalks, and add 2 large pieces of lemon peel and the lemon juice, along with the remaining 60 ml (4 tbsp) oil. Leave to marinate for 2–3 hours. Place the fish in a double-handled barbecue fish grill if you have one, or on a wire rack above the grid of the barbecue – the fish should cook very slowly, so you don't want direct heat on the flesh at this stage. Brush all surfaces which will touch the fish with oil, to prevent sticking. Place the rack over the barbecue and start cooking. After 10 minutes turn it round, and do so again 10 minutes later. It's a very slow process, particularly if the fish is stuffed. After about 35 minutes, check that the fish is cooked (see below). If not, cook directly on the barbecue grid, for a few more minutes – you don't want the fish to be overcooked. The backbone inside will be slightly pink still if it's cooked to perfection. Just before serving, take the fennel stalks used in the marinade and place them over the barbecue to toast lightly – this brings out their flavour. Place on a platter with the fish on top, and take to the table.

100 ml (4 fl oz) olive oil,
   infused with 20 ml (4 tsp)
   fennel seeds
fresh lemon quarters

Carve in front of your guests and serve with the strained olive oil, and fresh lemons.

TIP

The sense of touch is particularly valuable when cooking fish. When a whole fish is cooked to perfection, it will feel tender and offer a little resistance to the finger. (Raw fish will feel spongy and soft in varying degrees; overcooked fish hard and rubbery.) Feel the flesh near the tail. However, an easier method might be to pull at the base of the dorsal spine; if this comes out easily, the fish is cooked. Or, insert a thin metal skewer into the deep part of the flesh near the head: hold there for a second, and if the skewer is hot to the touch when withdrawn, the fish is ready.

WHOLE CHARCOAL-GRILLED SALMON TROUT

Other fish can be charcoal-grilled like the trout here, and the sea bass on page 136. Most oily fish – sardines, mackerel and herring, for instance – are delicious cooked on a barbecue, and I always prefer to cook the fish whole on the bone – it tastes so much better.

Serves 4

1 fresh salmon trout, about 1 kg (2¼ lb), scaled	Clean through the gills (see the Tip), and wash and rinse thoroughly until the water runs clear.
50 g (2 oz) butter, softened **20 g** (¾ oz) mixed fresh herbs (parsley, chervil, tarragon, basil, dill), finely cut **2** cloves garlic, crushed **15 ml** (1 tbsp) lemon juice salt and freshly ground pepper	Make a savoury butter by mixing all together, then pipe into the fish. Dry the skin well with kitchen paper.
50 ml (2 fl oz) herb oil (see page 205)	Brush over fish and grill as for the sea bass on page 136, for approximately 20 minutes, turning and brushing with oil from time to time. Test, as for sea bass, to check that it is cooked.

TIP
Round fish can be gutted through the gills as well as through the belly. Pull the gill flaps open and cut away the gills with kitchen scissors (1). Reach inside with a finger or, if necessary, a spoon to hook out the gills and intestines (2). The spinal cord should be removed too as it can be very bitter. Use the hooked handle of a ladle. Rinse under a tap until the water runs clear (from the rear vent), and then pat dry.

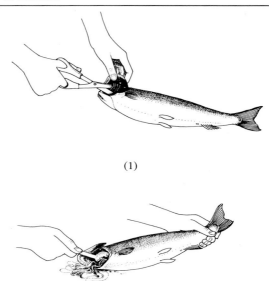

(1)

(2)

LEMON CHICKEN

This is a good recipe for taking on a picnic. Ensure that it is well chilled after cooking, and transport in a cool box. Serve with a selection of salads. (It can also be served hot, of course.)

Serves 8

8 chicken breasts on the bone	Trim and wipe.
2 lemons	For the marinade, zest the lemons, saving a large piece of peel for the sauce, then juice them.
2 litres (3½ pints) white chicken stock (see page 193) salt and freshly ground pepper	Place stock, lemon juice, zest and seasoning in a large enamelled or stainless steel pan, and bring to the boil. Add the chicken, and simmer for 8–10 minutes. Remove from the heat, quickly cool by putting the pan on ice, and marinate for about 3 hours. Remove the chicken from the stock and put to one side. Skim all the fat from the stock and pass through a fine cloth. Reduce the stock to two-thirds of its original volume by boiling.
1 clove **4** fresh mint leaves	Add to the stock with the reserved lemon peel, and reduce again to not less than 425 ml (¾ pint) for the sauce.
75 g (3 oz) each of carrots, leeks and celery, diced	Strain the stock, add the vegetables, and bring back to the boil. Taste and add seasoning if necessary. Remove skin from the chicken, and warm through in the sauce if serving hot. Otherwise, cover with the sauce when both are cooling, then chill when cold. The sauce will be slightly gelatinous.

SPINACH, LEEK AND CHEESE PIE

Another filo pastry pie which is slightly more substantial. Make it in a 25 cm (10 in) tin with a removable base.

Serves 8	Oven: moderately hot, 190°C/375°F/Gas 5
300 g (11 oz) white of leek	Cut in half lengthwise, rinse thoroughly and drain. Slice thinly.
4 spring onions, white part only	Trim and slice thinly.
45 ml (3-tbsp) olive oil	Heat in a heavy pan, and sauté leek and spring onion until softened but not browned.
675 g (1½ lb) small-leafed spinach, trimmed, washed, blanched and dried **2** garlic cloves, crushed freshly ground pepper	Increase heat and add, with pepper to taste. Cook uncovered for 2 minutes only. Remove from heat and drain in a colander, pressing out any excess liquid.
100 g (4 oz) good cooked ham, thickly sliced, then diced **25 g** (1 oz) fine fresh breadcrumbs	Stir ham and 15 ml (1 tbsp) of the breadcrumbs into the spinach mixture and allow to cool.
50 g (2 oz) unsalted butter	Melt and reserve.
2 eggs	Beat lightly in a large bowl.
100 g (4 oz) Gruyère cheese, grated **100 g** (4 oz) Gorgonzola cheese, crumbled **25 g** (1 oz) Parmesan cheese, grated **150 g** (5 oz) Ricotta cheese	Add to the eggs, along with the spinach mixture, and mix well.

10 sheets filo pastry (see page 202)

Unfold on a flat work surface and remove one sheet, covering the rest with a slightly damp teatowel.

Place sheet over the tin on a baking sheet, and brush carefully with melted butter, then sprinkle with some of the remaining breadcrumbs.

Continue stacking filo sheets in the same way, using four more sheets, brushing each with butter and crumbs.

Spoon spinach-cheese filling over the last filo sheet and cover with another sheet of filo. Brush with butter and sprinkle lightly with crumbs.

Continue this, using remaining four sheets of pastry. Leave last sheet bare of butter and crumbs.

Fold ends of sheets over the top of the pie in the tin to enclose filling.

Brush top of pie with remaining melted butter, and bake in the preheated oven for 20 minutes or until pie is golden brown.

TIP

The four cheeses used in this pie blend together to yield a very good flavour, but substitutes may be used. Instead of the Gorgonzola, try any good blue cheese, and Edam, Emmental or a mature Cheddar could be used instead of the Gruyère. A cottage cheese could be used instead of the Ricotta, and Sbrinz instead of the Parmesan.

STUFFED PEPPERS

Stuffed peppers are delicious hot as a light lunch or supper, but they are also good cold, and can be taken on a picnic in a suitable container. You could cook them the night before.

Serves 4

8 medium peppers, assorted red, orange, yellow, green	Cut a lid off the top of each, and remove the cores and seeds. Rinse well and drain.
2 onions, chopped **30 ml** (2 tbsp) olive oil	Sweat together in a shallow pan for a few minutes until soft. Allow to cool.
750 g (1 lb 10 oz) mixed lean pork and beef, minced **2** eggs, mixed with a fork **1** clove garlic, crushed approx **15 ml** (1 tbsp) mixed dried herbs (oregano, rosemary, sage, thyme etc) salt and freshly ground pepper	Mix into the onions, and season to taste. Fill the peppers with the meat mixture, replace the lids, and arrange in a fireproof pan, standing up side by side.
500 g (18 oz) tomatoes, finely chopped **200 ml** (7 fl oz) vegetable or chicken stock (see pages 192 and 193)	Place around the peppers, mixing well, and season. Cover and simmer for about 30 minutes on top of the stove. Remove the peppers carefully, and liquidise the sauce, then push through a fine sieve. It should be just spooning consistency; if too thin, boil to reduce a little.
4 large sprigs basil, cut thinly	Mix into the tomato just before serving.

TORTINO

This pizza-type tart, from the Mediterranean, may have a pastry or pizza dough base, and the topping ingredients can vary too, often including cheese and tomatoes. The tarts can be eaten hot or cold, thus are ideal for taking on picnics. Wrap with care.

Serves 8

Oven: very hot, 240°C/475°F/Gas 9

20 g (¾ oz) fresh yeast **175–200 ml** (6–7 fl oz) lukewarm milk	Dissolve the yeast in the milk.
175 g (6 oz) each of wheatmeal and white unbleached bread flours	Sift into a large bowl, and make a well in the centre.
125 ml (4½ fl oz) olive oil a pinch of salt	Add with the yeast milk, and mix everything together. Knead for a few minutes. Form the dough into a ball, and place in an oiled bowl. Cover with clingfilm and leave to rise in a warm place for 1 hour.
100 ml (4 fl oz) olive oil **300 g** (11 oz) onions, finely chopped	Meanwhile, make the topping. Sweat the onions in the oil in a large pan – do not brown.
3 cloves garlic **30 ml** (2 tbsp) capers, rinsed and drained	Crush together and add to the onions.
freshly ground pepper **5 ml** (1 tsp) finely chopped thyme	Season with pepper to taste and the thyme. When the dough has risen, knead again and roll out into a large pizza shape of about 3 mm (⅛ in) thick. Place on an oiled baking sheet and gently raise the edges.
12 anchovy fillets **150 g** (5 oz) black olives, pitted	Spread the onion mixture on the dough base, then arrange the anchovies across in a trellis pattern. Place an olive in each square. Bake in the preheated oven for 20 minutes.

VEGETABLES

Many vegetables can be cooked very successfully on the barbecue – either directly on the barbecue grid, or as kebabs, or wrapped in foil. I like to place them directly on to the grid, whole or sliced, which browns them and flavours them nicely. They need to be moistened with a seasoned herb oil though, to protect them a little from the searing heat – and some could benefit from a short marination. Brush the vegetables with the marinade using a new paintbrush. Vegetables also need to be watched carefully as they can, of course, overcook very easily. Try some of the following.

Aubergines (eggplants) Cut in thick slices, brush with oil, and cook for a maximum of 8–10 minutes. They look wonderful with the criss-cross pattern from the grid.

Carrots Use small new carrots, trimmed, or larger carrots, scrubbed and cut into thick slices lengthways. Brush with oil and grill for about 10–12 minutes.

Corn on the cob Cut small trimmed and cleaned cobs into chunks and brush very well with oil. Grill for about 8 minutes.

Courgettes Use smaller ones whole, larger ones cut in half lengthways. Brush with oil and grill, cut side down, for about 5–6 minutes.

Leeks Choose thin ones and trim off the root and most of the tough green leaves. Brush with oil and grill for about 8–10 minutes.

Mushrooms Large field mushrooms, painted well with thyme-scented oil, cook in seconds.

Onions Use the large Spanish ones. Peel and slice them thickly. Brush with oil and grill for about 8–10 minutes.

Peppers De-seed and trim and cut into chunky slices. Brush with oil and grill for 8–10 minutes.

Tomatoes Halve medium-sized tomatoes and cut beef tomatoes into thick slices. Brush with oil and grill very briefly.

Arrange your cooked vegetables decoratively on a large platter, and garnish with some fresh herb leaves to add colour. Season with salt and pepper and sprinkle over a little olive oil, preferably one flavoured with herbs. The vegetables may look a little dry, but they won't taste it.

Potatoes Baking potatoes can be wrapped in foil and cooked on top of the barbecue, but I prefer to cook smaller potatoes, or new potatoes, in a terracotta pot specially for the purpose. No fat is added, and the scrubbed potatoes 'bake' in the tightly closed pot on the barbecue with nothing added except some seasoning and a sprig of thyme. They take much longer than they would if boiled, but taste wonderfully earthy!

GREEN NOODLE SALAD

This salad could also be served as a starter dish. Turn the noodles in half the dressing while still warm, then make nests on four plates. Scatter over the tomato concasse, and place the seafood (turned separately in the other half of the dressing, then drained) on top. Pour the remaining dressing over.

Serves 4

225 g (8 oz) green noodles (see page 203) salt	Make as described on page 203, and then cook in boiling salted water for 2–3 minutes if fresh, double that time if dry. Leave to cool in a bowl.
100 g (4 oz) tomato concasse (see page 198) **200 g** (7 oz) cooked, still warm, seafood, mixed or to taste (shrimps, mussels etc)	Mix gently into the noodles.
salt and freshly ground pepper **15 ml** (1 tbsp) sherry vinegar **75 ml** (5 tbsp) sunflower oil **15 ml** (1 tbsp) sesame oil **15 ml** (1 tbsp) red wine vinegar	Make a dressing by mixing together well in the order given.
30 ml (2 tbsp) cooking liquor from seafood (optional)	Add a little to the dressing to dilute it to taste, then dress the salad.
20 g (¾ oz) sesame seeds, freshly roasted	Scatter over the top of the salad, and serve immediately.

RICE SALAD

Wild rice is actually not a rice at all, but the seeds of a North American water grass. It's deliciously nutty in flavour, and is becoming much more widely available in supermarkets and good food shops. Make the salad the day before and keep chilled, to serve at barbecues, picnics or at buffet parties.

Serves 4

80 g (3¼ oz) wild rice, rinsed and drained	Bring a large pan of salted water to the boil and stir in the rice. Boil for 15 minutes.
100 g (4 oz) brown rice, rinsed and drained	Add, stir and boil for a further 10 minutes.
50 g (2 oz) white rice	Add, stir and cook for a further 8 minutes. Drain the rices in a colander and rinse under cold running water. Set the colander *over* a pan of boiling water, cover with a cloth and lid, and steam for 15–20 minutes until rice is fluffy, tender and dry. Transfer to a large bowl.
salt and freshly ground pepper **50 ml** (2 fl oz) sherry vinegar **100 ml** (4 fl oz) olive oil	To make a dressing, dissolve salt and pepper to taste in the vinegar, then add the oil gradually, whisking constantly. Pour over the rice and mix.
12 black olives, pitted **50 g** (2 oz) spring onions, finely sliced **15 g** (½ oz) Italian parsley, finely cut	Add, with more salt and pepper to taste, and fold lightly to combine.
4 white chicory spears	Use to garnish the salad.

TIP

There are as many ways of cooking rice as there are varieties of rice. Some rices need to be washed, some need to be soaked; some are cooked in excess water then drained, some are cooked in a precise amount of water which is absorbed by the rice. In many cuisines, when rice is almost cooked, it is steamed to finish the cooking and to fluff and dry it. The Turks use a special cushion as a lid, and the Indians use a cloth between pot and lid for their *pullaos*. The purpose of this is to seal the saucepan as tightly as possible and to absorb extra moisture from the condensation.

COUSCOUS SALAD

Couscous is a wheat semolina product most famous as the national dish of Morocco. It is available in supermarkets and health-food shops. The salad can be made a day ahead, as long as it is covered and chilled, and is ideal for both picnics and barbecues.

Serves 6

Ingredients	Method
40 g (1½ oz) unsalted butter a good pinch of saffron, infused in 30 ml (2 tbsp) water **350 ml** (12 fl oz) vegetable or chicken stock (see pages 192 and 193)	Melt the butter in a suitable pan, then add the saffron and stock and bring to the boil.
250 g (9 oz) couscous	Stir in, cover, and remove from the heat. Let stand for 10–12 minutes, then transfer to a bowl, breaking up lumps with a fork. (The grains should have absorbed all the liquid.)
100 g (4 oz) celery, trimmed and finely diced **75 g** (3 oz) seedless raisins, soaked in water **1** bunch spring onions, thinly sliced **75 g** (3 oz) pine nuts, lightly toasted **15 g** (½ oz) parsley, finely chopped	Add, and toss to mix.
2 lemons, juiced a pinch of powdered cinnamon **100 ml** (4 fl oz) olive oil, warmed slightly	Make a dressing by mixing together the lemon juice and cinnamon, then adding the oil gradually, whisking constantly.
salt and freshly ground pepper	Pour the dressing over the salad, toss and season with salt and pepper to taste.

MARINATED ROASTED PEPPERS

These peppers are ideal for any sort of outdoor eating, particularly for a picnic, as they have to be left to marinate for at least twelve hours.

Serves 8

Oven: moderately hot, 200°C/400°F/Gas 6

800 g (1¾ lb) peppers, preferably green, red and yellow

Cut in half and remove seeds and white cores.
Place pepper halves side by side on a baking tray, skin downwards. Bake for about 30 minutes then turn over and bake for a further 15 minutes.

4 cloves garlic
3 very thin slices fresh chilli (optional)
15 ml (1 tbsp) finely chopped oregano
50 ml (2 fl oz) white wine vinegar
175 ml (6 fl oz) olive oil
salt and freshly ground pepper

Meanwhile make a spicy dressing. Crush two of the garlic cloves and mix with all the remaining ingredients.
Remove the peppers from the oven and spray with cold water, after which they can be easily peeled.
Cut each piece in half and place in a dish (or the picnic container).
Pour the dressing over the warm peppers, add the peeled remaining garlic, and marinate overnight.

45 ml (3 tbsp) finely chopped parsley

Mix in just before serving.

TIP
If you sprinkle each layer of vegetables with dressing, the peppers will absorb the flavours within 3–4 hours. The peppers are also delicious if served with a small bowl of black Provençal olives, about 6 oz (175 g), marinated in a further quantity of the dressing with the addition of 4 sprigs of fresh thyme.

RATATOUILLE

This summer dish – one of the best – is suitable for the family or for a large group of guests. It can be served straight from the oven, or, on hot summer days, is nice lukewarm. It also tastes delicious as a cold salad if taken on a picnic. All that is needed is garlic bread, or a plain fresh *baguette* and a light dry wine.

Serves 8	**Oven:** moderately hot, 200°C/400°F/Gas 6
500 g (18 oz) small aubergines	Dice. If larger, 'degorge' as in the Tip.
8 small button onions, blanched	Peel and cut in half.
4 peppers, green, red and yellow, washed	Halve, remove seeds, and cut into pieces.
500 g (18 oz) small courgettes, washed and trimmed	Cut in half lengthwise, then across into 3 cm (1¼ in) pieces.
1 kg (2¼ lb) fleshy tomatoes, seeded	Roughly dice.
1 bunch spring onions	Clean, and cut into rings.
90 ml (6 tbsp) olive oil **4** cloves garlic, unskinned and crushed **1** sprig thyme **1** bay leaf	Heat the oil, infusing with the garlic and herbs. Soften each vegetable slowly, one at a time, in the oil, beginning with the button onions, following with the peppers, courgettes, tomatoes, spring onions and aubergines last. Add more oil as necessary. Drain all the vegetables in a colander after frying, and catch the juices to return to the pan. Place all vegetables and juices in a casserole.
150 ml (¼ pint) vegetable stock (see page 192)	Use to deglaze the frying pan, then add to the vegetables.
salt and freshly ground pepper	Season well, and cook on the lowest shelf of the oven, covered, for about 15 minutes. Strain the liquid and boil to reduce, then add the vegetables. Remove the garlic before serving.
½ bunch flat-leaf parsley	Arrange in fronds around the side of the dish.

TIP

If the aubergines are large, and fat, 'degorge' by sprinkling the dice with salt in a colander. Leave while preparing all the other vegetables, and bitter juices will run out. Rinse and dry.

TIP

For extra flavour and texture, before baking you could sprinkle the tops of the breads with seeds – try poppy or sesame – or with wheat flakes or cracked wheat.

FLOWERPOT BREAD WITH ONIONS

Flowerpots make good baking moulds – very appropriate for bread to be eaten outside at a barbecue or picnic! Wash new clay flowerpots of about 12–15 cm (5–6 in) in diameter, 12 cm (5 in) deep, and allow to dry well. Brush inside and outside with plenty of oil, then heat on a baking sheet for 30 minutes at 220°C/425°F/Gas 7. Repeat this several times. The pots will give off a lot of smoke. Allow to cool then line with aluminium foil.

Makes 2 loaves, enough for 10 people

Oven: moderately hot, 190°C/375°F/Gas 5

450 g (1 lb) white unbleached bread flour, plus extra for dusting and kneading
2 pinches sugar
2 pinches salt

Sift together into a bowl.

15 g (½ oz) fresh yeast
175 ml (6 fl oz) lukewarm skimmed milk
125 ml (4½ fl oz) lukewarm water

In another bowl, mix the fresh yeast with a little of the lukewarm milk, then add the remaining milk and the water.
Work in half the measured flour, sprinkle with a little of the extra flour, then cover the bowl with a damp teatowel and leave in a warm place for 15 minutes to rise to a froth. Work the remaining measured flour gradually into the risen dough until it comes away from the sides of the bowl. On a lightly floured board, knead the warm dough for 10–15 minutes until smooth and shiny, or use a dough hook or food processor.

15 ml (1 tbsp) vegetable oil

Brush a bowl with a little of the oil, and place the dough in it. Cover with clingfilm and leave to rise in a warm place for 1–1½ hours, or until tripled in size.

100 g (4 oz) onion, finely chopped

Meanwhile, sauté lightly in the remaining oil. Drain well on kitchen paper, then add onion to the risen dough. Knead well.
Divide the dough into two equal pieces. Knead each into a ball and place in the foil-lined flowerpots (see above). Cover and leave to rise again in a warm place for 30 minutes.

1 egg, beaten
5 ml (1 tsp) salt

Beat together and brush very gently over the top of the dough – it's very fragile at this stage. Sprinkle with seeds if you like (see below).
Bake in the preheated oven for about 40 minutes until well browned. To test if the bread is cooked, remove from the pot and tap the base. It will sound hollow when cooked.

ITALIAN PICNIC BREAD

Before the pizza became what it is today, it was a simple country pancake bread. It goes well with wine and with *hors d'oeuvre*, and is also handy to carry on a picnic, ideal for eating with summery salads.

Serves 10	**Oven:** hot, 220°C/425°F/Gas 7
300 g (11 oz) white unbleached bread flour	Place in a bowl and make a well in the centre.
15 g (½ oz) fresh yeast **200 ml** (7 fl oz) lukewarm water	Dissolve the yeast in half the water and add to the well. Mix in gradually until a dough is formed, knead and leave to rise in a warm oiled bowl in a warm place covered with oiled polythene, for about 45 minutes.
at least **60 ml** (4 tbsp) olive oil salt	Add 45 ml (3 tbsp) of the oil, a little salt and the remaining water, and work to a firm dough. Allow to rise to twice its volume as above, about 45 minutes, then knead again.
15 ml (1 tbsp) fresh rosemary **10** small sage leaves **1–2** sprigs thyme **15 ml** (1 tbsp) dry white wine	Wash the herbs, dry between kitchen paper, then chop. Mix into the wine and work into the dough. Divide the dough in half and form into two thick rounds.
sea salt flakes	Oil a baking tray and sprinkle lightly with salt flakes. Place the dough rounds on it, and brush them with oil. Cover with oiled polythene, put in a warm, moist place, and allow to rise again, about 15 minutes. Bake in the preheated oven for 10–15 minutes, or until golden and crisp.

QUARK PURÉE

Quark is a slightly astringent fromage blanc which has no fat at all, therefore makes a very healthy ingredient of a great many puddings and pastries. (Fromage blanc is a fresh, low-fat cheese which is used in sauces etc.) This purée is very light, especially at the end of a barbecue meal consisting of many courses!

Serves 10

350 g (12 oz) blackberries, or half and half blackberries and blueberries	Purée, reserving a few for decoration.
850 g (1 lb 14 oz) quark (see page 200)	Pass the berry purée through a stainless steel sieve and mix well with the quark.
1 lemon, juiced caster or icing sugar to taste 4 sprigs mint	Add the lemon juice and sweeten with sugar to taste. Spoon into a bowl or dish, and decorate with the reserved berries and the mint.

CARROT CAKE

Buy the icing and marzipan to mould into cake topping and carrots respectively – or the cake can simply be decorated with a dusting of icing sugar. Apricot glaze is lump-free or sieved apricot jam, boiled with a little water until it falls in slow sticky drops from a spoon.

Serves 10	**Oven:** moderate, 180°C/350°F/Gas 4
2 lemons	Finely zest both lemons, and squeeze the juice from one.
6 eggs, separated **300 g** (11 oz) caster sugar	Beat the yolks in a large bowl with half the caster sugar, the lemon juice and zest until pale and sticky.
300 g (11 oz) carrots, finely grated **300 g** (11 oz) ground almonds	Fold in carefully.
75 g (3 oz) cornflour a pinch of powdered cinnamon **10 g** (¼ oz) baking powder	Sift together, and fold in lightly with a spatula. Whisk the egg whites until stiff, and fold in the rest of the sugar. Carefully fold this into the carrot mixture. Place in a prepared 25 cm (10 in) cake tin and bake in the preheated oven for 1 hour. Test to see that it's cooked by feeling the centre. It should spring back when pressed lightly. Turn out of tin.
150 g (5 oz) apricot glaze	When cool, brush over the cake. Allow to set.
150 g (5 oz) fondant icing marzipan carrots	Cover with icing, and decorate with carrots.

TIP
To prepare a cake tin, brush it well inside with soft butter. Some cakes require a bottom lining so that the cake will not stick and will slip out easily, and this is easy to do whether the tin is round or square, or indeed of any fancy shape. Stand the tin on a piece of greaseproof or parchment paper and pencil round the base. Cut out the pencilled shape slightly inside the pencil line, and it should fit perfectly. Insert in the tin and butter the paper as well.

BANANAS IN FOIL

These are extremely simple but so delicious. It is vital to take the hot parcels to the guests and cut them open with scissors in front of them, so that they can appreciate to the full the wonderful aroma of the cinnamon and vanilla.

Simply use one banana per person (they can be a bit bruised, it's a good way of using them up), and slice in half lengthwise. Lay the halves on buttered foil in one layer, and sprinkle with a little brown sugar. Put in a piece of whole cinnamon, a small section of a vanilla pod, a couple of grapefruit or orange segments plus some grapefruit or orange juice, along with some lemon juice.

Fold over the edges of the foil to make a puffed but tightly sealed parcel. Lay directly on the barbecue grid and heat through for about 10–12 minutes. If the packets bubble it's a good sign that they are airtight.

Serve garnished with mint leaves.

SUMMER PUDDING LYN HALL

I didn't encounter summer pudding until I came to England, but it is a firm favourite now. I have adapted it, though, making it with brown bread which is healthier than white, and with very much *less* bread and more fruit than is normal. Yoghurt too is used for decoration, as it is obviously healthier than cream. It all works wonderfully. Not to be transported too far – a table in the garden, I would suggest – but it can be wrapped carefully, and unmoulded just before serving.

Serves 8

5 ml (1 tsp) oil	Brush a 850 ml (1½ pint) pudding basin lightly with oil.
8 large thin slices wholemeal bread, crusts removed	Cut the bread into tapered rectangles, and line the basin with some of the bread.
4 leaves gelatine, soaked in cold water and squeezed dry **100 ml** (4 fl oz) water **1** lemon, juiced	Dissolve the gelatine in the water over a gentle heat, then stir in the lemon juice. Strain and divide this liquid between three small stainless steel pans.

200 g (7 oz) each of ripe strawberries, raspberries and blackberries (or blueberries)	Add the strawberries, raspberries and blackberries (or blueberries) separately to these three amounts of liquid and stew gently until just tender – just until their juices start to run, but they are still holding their shape, and are a rich colour. Handle them with love and care. Place alternate layers of the individual fruits and bread in the basin, finishing with a layer of any fruit that is left, mixed, along with some juice if necessary. Top with the last two slices of bread. Cover with a saucer or a round piece of cardboard wrapped in foil – and weight down with something heavy (a large can of fruit, for instance). Allow to set in the refrigerator for at least 12 hours so that the juice can soak through the bread.
400 g (14 oz) raspberries **60 ml** (4 tbsp) icing sugar **1** small lemon, juiced	For the sauce, press the raspberries through a sieve, and mix with the sugar and lemon juice. Unmould the pudding on to the centre of a serving plate and carefully pour the sauce over the top of the pudding to cover it completely. Spoon from the plate to give a good glossy finish.
50 g (2 oz) natural yoghurt *or* **50 ml** (2 fl oz) whipped cream	Fill a small greaseproof-paper piping bag (see Tip) with the yoghurt or cream, and snip off the end. Pipe circles of yoghurt around the top of the pudding and, if you wish, around the outside edge of the sauce-covered plate. Then, using a toothpick, draw the yoghurt through the sauce to give a decorative finish.
seasonal whole fruit – pairs of cherries on the stalk, raspberries, blueberries, bilberries, or whitecurrants mint sprigs icing sugar	Top the pudding with some fruit and/or mint leaves, and decorate the edges of the plate with fruit and whirls of yoghurt as well. As a final touch, you could sift a little icing sugar over the top of the pudding.

TIP
To make a piping bag, cut a 25 cm (10 in) square piece of greaseproof paper. Fold the square in half diagonally and cut into two triangles (1). Holding the right-angled apex of one triangle in one hand, bend one of the other corners round to meet the apex, followed by the other, to give a double thickness cone shape (2). Slide the three top points together between index finger and thumb until the point becomes watertight and sharp. Fold them down to hold the cone together and the point rigid (3). When filled and folded over, cut off a tiny tip at the end of the cone (4).

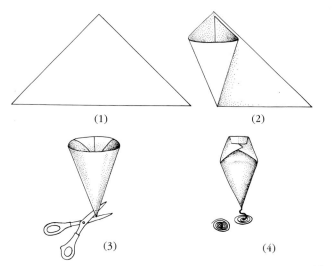

(1) (2) (3) (4)

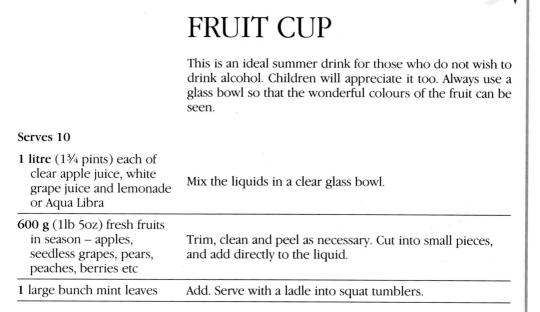

FRUIT CUP

This is an ideal summer drink for those who do not wish to drink alcohol. Children will appreciate it too. Always use a glass bowl so that the wonderful colours of the fruit can be seen.

Serves 10

1 litre (1¾ pints) each of clear apple juice, white grape juice and lemonade or Aqua Libra	Mix the liquids in a clear glass bowl.
600 g (1lb 5oz) fresh fruits in season – apples, seedless grapes, pears, peaches, berries etc	Trim, clean and peel as necessary. Cut into small pieces, and add directly to the liquid.
1 large bunch mint leaves	Add. Serve with a ladle into squat tumblers.

FRUIT BOWL

This is a wonderfully refreshing – and not too alcoholic – brew which is a perfect accompaniment to barbecued food.

Serves 4

400 g (14 oz) mixed fruits as above	Trim, clean and peel as necessary, and cut into small pieces. Place all but the berries in a bowl.
60 g (2½ oz) sugar **60 ml** (4 tbsp) brandy a dash of lime juice	Pour over, and leave to macerate for several hours in a cold place, covered tightly with clingfilm.
1 bottle chilled champagne or ½ bottle dry white wine and ½ bottle mineral water	Just before serving, transfer to a large glass bowl. Add the berries and fill up with champagne (or wine and mineral water). Serve immediately.

DINNER AT MOSIMANN'S

It was in November 1978, when I was Maître-Chef des Cuisines at the Dorchester, that I first presented my 'Menu Surprise'. This was a dinner of six courses, with the guest not knowing what he would eat until each course appeared on the table. The thinking behind it was that it would make the best use of the freshest seasonal ingredients in the market that day, and it was heralded as something completely unique in restaurant dining. The London *Evening Standard* dubbed it 'culinary blind dating', and that this concept appealed to many guests was reflected in the ever-increasing numbers who opted over the next ten years to be 'surprised'!

It is fun to go out to eat in a restaurant without knowing what you will get; many guests enjoy being freed of the burden of choice, and for the chef it is also a good way of encouraging guests to taste things they might be shy of ordering, for instance oysters and wild duck. It is also an enjoyable challenge for the chef, who is not only able to cook, for once, what he considers best, but he can also present a complete and balanced *menu*, which will be much more representative of his culinary skills, rather than a disparate selection of dishes.

Menu planning in itself is an art, and to combine a menu is like composing a symphony: everything must be in harmony. Even at home this should apply, whether you are serving a basic three-course meal or a more ambitious six- or seven-course feast. Simplicity should be the keynote, avoiding unnecessary complications: a simple menu, simple preparations and simple natural flavours are not only the most relaxed and healthy to achieve, they are also the most up-to-date rule of cooking. The art of menu planning is common sense, in a way, but involves many facets. The chosen courses must complement each other in terms of flavours, colours, quality and quantity of ingredients. If you start off with something too strong in flavour, for instance, your guests may not taste anything else in the rest of the meal, so it is important to have the tastes balanced. A too lavish use of herbs can have the same effect, which is why the baby lamb in the dinner I chose to serve is garnished very simply. If you serve courses that are too substantial you can jade the palates of your guests just as much: there should be a balance in quantity just as in flavour. You want your guests to rise saying, '*What* a lovely meal' after a selection of light courses, feeling satisfied rather than sated.

165

Colour and presentation are vitally important too. Each dish should be like a work of art, the different elements arranged like a still-life, using the fresh colours of ingredients like colours in a paintbox. Unlike many chefs, I personally prefer to serve food directly on to the plate: this way *I* can 'art-direct', or control the detail on every plate. For how the food *looks* is the first impression it gives, although anything that looks good has to taste better.

In 1988, after thirteen happy years, I left the Dorchester and opened Mosimann's, a dining club in what was once The Belfry, which in its earliest incarnation had been a Scottish Presbyterian church. There I still serve my Menu Surprise – although I'm afraid it's a little more expensive than its original 1978 £24 for two! And it was at Mosimann's that I gave a dinner party for ten, with the Menu Surprise that follows. The guests were Trevor Hughes, wine merchant, and his wife Martine; merchant banker Bill Taylor and his wife Betty; hotelier and entrepreneur Bob Payton and his wife Wendy; Matt Aitken, record producer, and his friend Kate Williams; my wife Kathrin and myself. Although my appearances at the dining table in the Gucci room were somewhat infrequent – I was not only cooking, but the proceedings were being filmed at the same time – it was all great fun, and I'm sure everyone enjoyed the meal.

The dinner party took place in March, and thus the centre-piece was the wonderful new spring lamb from Kent, simply roasted. At this time it is at its peak, with beautifully white and tender flesh. With that I served the tiny Jersey potatoes which come in just before the first crop of mainland early potatoes. The 'gourmandises' which preceded the lamb featured many seasonal delicacies – scallops and leeks, for instance – and all were in such tiny portions that they would not detract from the glories to follow. The sorbets, served before the main dessert, featured the early forced rhubarb so tender at that time of year. Other sorbets and the *pièce de résistance* of the desserts – my passion fruit soufflé – were made from more exotic fruit, now available throughout the year. I also, I must admit, served my bread and butter pudding (see page 57). Despite its one-time nursery associations, it is an ideal dinner-party dessert, light and flavourful.

It was a carefully pre-planned meal, which incorporated all my philosophies of cooking – of lightness, of health, of balance and of presentation. Usually I have to imagine the appreciation of my guest when he first sees and then tastes the dishes. That evening I was able to experience at first hand the pleasure of my guests – and you should be able to experience this at home too. My profession, which I first chose to follow at the age of seven, is one of love and of giving, and whether I am preparing a meal for two, ten or a hundred, I can't think of anything I would rather be doing than creating and giving that pleasure.

Menu

Les Gourmandises Palace

Elixir de Volaille aux
Feuilles d'Or

Agneau de Kent Rôti aux
Herbes du Printemps

Pommes de Jersey Croustillant
avec un Petit Secret

Ratatouille en Pâte Filo

Selection of Cheeses

Bread and Butter Pudding

Symphonie de Sorbet

Soufflé aux Fruits de la Passion

Café et Délices des Dames

LES GOURMANDISES PALACE

These are a selection of tiny items, with a galaxy of flavours, something to everyone's taste, to be served as a starter. A few require quite detailed work, but they can be prepared in the morning and chilled before you arrange them artistically on individual plates, an hour or so before serving. I served six at my special dinner party, but you can of course serve fewer – just make the individual servings a little larger to compensate.

MARINATED SCALLOPS WITH ARTICHOKE AND MUSHROOM SALAD

Serves 10

5 large (or 10 medium) live scallops, freshly removed from shell	Separate coral from the white *noix*. Clean away the frills, membranes and sand. Rinse briefly and pat dry. Cut *noix* in half horizontally, or in 6 mm (¼ in) slices if large and fat. (Use the corals in another dish.)
5 ml (1 tsp) each of green peppercorns and capers, rinsed and well drained	Finely chop, and scatter half of the mixture on a large shallow plate.
1 lime, juiced **100 ml** (4 fl oz) olive oil	Mix the juice with two-thirds of the oil in a bowl and moisten the plate with it. Place the scallop slices in the marinade, turn once to coat with some of the mixture, and keep flat. Leave for 5–10 minutes, and turn again just before serving.
salt and freshly ground pepper **30 ml** (2 tbsp) finely cut chives	Taste scallops for seasoning, and sprinkle with half the chives.
4 cooked artichoke hearts (see Tip), halved and sliced **10** button mushrooms, wiped and finely sliced	Mix together for the salad.
10 ml (2 tsp) lemon juice	Season the salad to taste with salt, pepper, lemon juice and the remaining oil and chives. Arrange the salad on a plate with the scallops on top.

TIP

To prepare artichoke hearts, snap off the stem to pull out most of the tough fibres (1), then remove all the tough outside leaves one by one until you are left with the small tender centre leaves (2). With a large, sharp stainless steel knife, cut off the top part horizontally, removing about three-quarters of the whole (3). Trim the hearts, removing the tough base of the outer leaves (4), then remove the hairy chokes with a teaspoon (5). Rub with lemon and keep in cold lemon water until required (6).

In a stainless steel or enamelled pan, bring to the boil some water containing about 15 ml (1 tbsp) lemon juice, a little olive oil and some salt. Add the artichokes and blanch for 3–4 minutes. Then bring fresh water to the boil with up to 7.5 ml (½ tbsp) lemon juice and some salt. Add the artichokes, cover and simmer until soft. Allow to cool in the stock. (This double cooking ensures that the artichokes remain white, and also improves their flavour.)

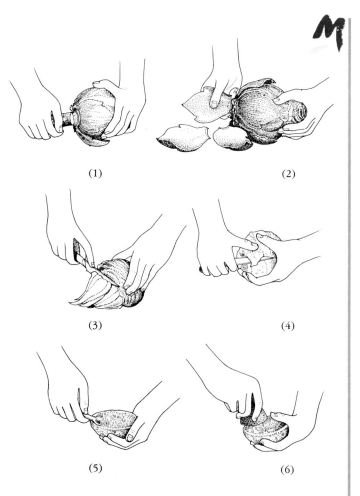

(1)   (2)   (3)   (4)   (5)   (6)

ROULADE OF SMOKED SALMON

Makes about 20 little roulades

250 g (9 oz) fresh salmon fillet, without skin	Place on a large piece of clingfilm.
7.5 ml (½ tbsp) salt **7.5 ml** (½ tbsp) caster sugar ½ lemon, zested and juiced **15 ml** (1 tbsp) snipped chives	Mix together everything except the lemon juice, and press carefully on to both sides of the fish. Sprinkle over 15 ml (1 tbsp) of the lemon juice, and wrap securely in the clingfilm. Leave in the refrigerator for 12–24 hours.
175 g (6 oz) smoked salmon fillet, sliced very thinly	Cut the smoked salmon into 7.5 cm (3 in) wide strips. Unwrap the marinated salmon and chop it very finely. Spread this salmon 'tartare' along the centre of the strips of smoked salmon. Roll up neatly and cut into 5 cm (2 in) lengths. Chill until ready to serve.

PARFAIT OF CHICKEN LIVER

Serves 10

2 medium shallots, sliced **250 g** (9 oz) unsalted butter	Sweat the shallots in 50 g (2 oz) of the butter without colouring.
250 g (9 oz) chicken livers, trimmed of all membranes, threads and any green parts salt and freshly ground pepper	Season, add to the pan, and turn the heat up. Sauté quickly.
75 ml (3 fl oz) port **45 ml** (3 tbsp) Madeira	Add and flame, then simmer to reduce slightly, making sure the chicken liver is still pink. Pour into a liquidiser or processor.
1 sprig marjoram	Add with the remaining butter, and process well.
2.5 ml (½ tsp) finely chopped truffle (optional) freshly grated nutmeg	Add, and season to taste. Pour the mixture into a suitable glass or china dish. Leave to cool and settle slightly before chilling.
50 g (2 oz) mixed vegetables (French beans, carrots and leek), cooked and finely diced	Sprinkle on top of the parfait.
250 ml (9 fl oz) chicken aspic (see Tip)	Coat the top of the parfait with some of the aspic, to cover the vegetable dice. Chill until needed, then serve by cutting into little egg shapes (coquilles) with the tip of a hot wet dessertspoon.

TIP
To make a chicken aspic, soften 2 leaves of gelatine in cold water, then squeeze dry. Dissolve in 250 ml (9 fl oz) warm chicken consommé (see page 174). Leave until the consistency of raw egg white before spooning on to the parfait.

LEEK AND CREAM CHEESE PARCELS

Makes 10 parcels

5 large leeks, trimmed and cleaned salt	Cook in boiling, salted water for 3–4 minutes. They should be tender, but still retain their colour. Refresh and drain well. Separate the layers. Cut the slightly tougher outer layers into 'strings', and keep about 20 of the outer-middle leaves as wrapping. Cut the hearts of the leeks finely.
200 g (7 oz) cream cheese or fromage blanc, drained **30 ml** (2 tbsp) finely cut chives	Mix into the finely cut leeks.
lemon juice cayenne pepper freshly ground pepper	Season the mixture to taste. For each parcel you need a wrapping of about 5 × 2.5 cm (2 × 1 in), so two leek leaves together may be necessary. Lay flat on a clean working surface. Place a dessertspoonful of cheese mixture in the middle of the leaves. Fold the leaves over as though wrapping a parcel. Trim and tie with leek 'strings'.
15 ml (1 tbsp) each of finely diced yellow and red pepper **30 ml** (2 tbsp) red wine vinegar **60 ml** (4 tbsp) safflower oil **15 ml** (1 tbsp) walnut oil **15 ml** (1 tbsp) chicken or vegetable stock (optional) salt and freshly ground pepper	Mix together and season to make a red and yellow pepper vinaigrette to serve with the leek parcels.

QUAILS' EGGS WITH SOURED CREAM AND CAVIAR

Serves 10

10 quails' eggs	To soft-boil, place in a sieve or blanching basket and plunge into boiling water. Cook for 1 minute then remove, place in cold water and peel (see Tip). Cut a tiny slice off the base of each egg, to help them stand up.
10 salad leaves (lollo rosso, rocket or curly endive), washed and dried	Arrange each on individual plates and rest an egg on top.
60 ml (4 tbsp) soured cream salt and freshly ground pepper	Season the cream and spoon a little over the top of each egg.
50 g (2 oz) caviar	Spoon a little over the top of the cream.

TIP
Quails' eggs have a tough skin or membrane beneath the shell. Tap the shell all over to break, then gently pierce the membrane with something sharp. Peel off the membrane and the egg shell will come away too.

Variation

Baked Potatoes with
Soured Cream and Caviar
Instead of the quails' eggs, you could use a tiny baked potato. Bake small new Jersey potatoes, one per person, as on page 44. Season soured cream to taste (you could add some snipped chives and lemon juice as well). Make an incision lengthwise in the potatoes and press them open slightly with your hands. Spoon in some flavoured soured cream. Top with a little caviar.

M

CUCUMBER AND CHERRY TOMATO SALAD

Serves 10

1 medium cucumber	Thinly peel and cut into batons approximately 4 cm × 6 mm (1½ × ¼ in). You need 40 pieces.
salt and freshly ground pepper **10 ml** (2 tsp) sherry vinegar **30 ml** (2 tbsp) grapeseed oil (or similar) **15 ml** (1 tbsp) finely cut dill	Season cucumber with salt and a little pepper, vinegar, oil and dill just to moisten.
10 cherry tomatoes, red, sweet and ripe, wiped	Arrange a tomato in the centre of four cucumber batons on individual plates.
50 g (2 oz) plain yoghurt **15 g** (½ oz) salmon eggs **10** tiny sprigs dill	Top each tomato with about 5 ml (1 tsp) plain yoghurt, a few salmon eggs and a tiny sprig of dill.

ELIXIR DE VOLAILLE AUX FEUILLES D'OR

This chicken consommé with edible gold leaf caused a sensation when I first served it about ten years ago. The headlines read, 'Gold being eaten at the Dorchester!'

Serves 4–6

2 raw chicken carcasses (about 900 g/2 lb)	Blanch in boiling water for 1 minute, then remove and rinse under cold running water.
30 ml (2 tbsp) groundnut oil	Heat in a large saucepan, and gently fry the carcasses until well browned. Drain off the fat.
1.5 litres (2½ pints) water salt	Add water, season sparingly with salt, and bring to the boil. Skim and allow to simmer for 10 minutes. Skim as required.
40 g (1½ oz) onion (with skin) **1 clove** ½ bay leaf	Brown the cut side of the onion under a grill or over direct heat. Stick onion with the clove and bay leaf.
½ small carrot ½ small leek ½ small celery stalk	Add to the stock with the onion, and simmer for a further 45 minutes, skimming from time to time. Pass the stock through a cloth-lined fine sieve, and allow to cool. Remove any traces of fat by dragging strips of kitchen paper across the surface of the consommé.
200 g (7 oz) raw poultry meat, coarsely minced or finely cut **2 egg whites**, whisked until frothy **50 g** (2 oz) tomatoes, coarsely chopped **50 g** (2 oz) trimmed celery, finely chopped a few parsley and tarragon stalks	To clarify the consommé, first mix all together. Add to the stock and bring to the boil, stirring constantly. Reduce the heat (or draw the pan to the side), and allow to simmer gently for 20 minutes undisturbed.
salt and freshly ground pepper	When the stock is sparkling clear, season with salt and pepper, then pass slowly and carefully through fine muslin into a clean pan. Again, remove all fat as before.
sheets of edible gold leaf	To serve, reheat gently, pour into small soup cups, and cover each with a square of gold leaf.

TIPS
The best stock results from using fresh and raw chicken carcasses. When jointing a chicken for its legs, wings and boned breasts, you could freeze the carcass for making a stock at a future time.

Pure gold and silver leaf is found in good Indian food suppliers, and in shops selling artists' requirements. The leaf is used in India to decorate celebratory *birianis*, the luxurious rice dishes beloved of the Moghul emperors.

AGNEAU DE KENT RÔTI AUX HERBES DU PRINTEMPS

A roast, of whatever size, of the new season's spring lamb, needs very little done to it – just simply roasted, it will taste magnificent. A whole lamb weighs about 7.2 kg (16 lb), and it is then divided into the various cuts. The best joints for roasting are the two shoulders, two legs, and the loin or saddle. Keep the bones and roast them earlier to make a gravy (see Tip below). A whole lamb may seem a bit of an extravagance, but spring lamb *is* very small! To cater for numbers different to those here, calculate on buying about 350–400 g (12–14 oz) per person on the bone.

Serves 10

Oven: hot, 220°C/425°F/Gas 7

2 legs of lamb, trimmed (about 1.4–1.8 kg/3–4 lb each) 2 shoulders of lamb, boned and tied (about 900 g/2 lb each) 1 saddle of lamb, tied (about 1.8 kg/4 lb) groundnut oil salt and freshly ground pepper	Heat a little oil in a large roasting tray or pan on top of the stove. Season the meat and place in the pan one by one to seal and colour on all sides. Place in the preheated oven and roast for approximately 15 minutes. Reduce the temperature to 200°C/400°F/Gas 6, and continue roasting for a further 10 minutes, basting occasionally. Check the meat. The shoulder and saddle should be ready and still pink; the legs will need another 10 minutes or so. Keep all the meat together, and leave in a warm place to rest, for up to 45 minutes, while you finish the gravy (see Tip).
20 g (¾ oz) Dijon mustard 20 g (¾ oz) grain mustard	Mix together, then brush over the shoulders and saddle.
200 g (7 oz) parsley, chopped	Roll mustard-covered meats in the parsley.
80 g (3¼ oz) butter 2 large sprigs rosemary	Heat together until butter starts to turn brown and frothy. Remove from heat and pour over the legs. Carve meat and serve with vegetables and gravy.

TIP

To make the lamb gravy, you will have to start at least a couple of hours before you wish to serve. A good lamb stock from the bones takes time and the lamb takes less than an hour to cook! Pre-roast the chopped bones as for the beef gravy on page 43, and then follow exactly the same procedure (but using water or lamb stock). When the lamb is finally taken from the oven, remove all the fat from the roasting tin, deglaze the tin with a few ladlefuls of the lamb stock, then strain and correct seasoning and consistency.

POMMES DE JERSEY CROUSTILLANT AVEC UN PETIT SECRET

The flavours of tiny new potatoes are enhanced by the 'secret', the subtle earthy taste of mushrooms. Use whatever you can find in the market; the varieties which are offered are increasing rapidly. Both wild, cultivated or the large field mushrooms go very well with the plainly cooked lamb.

Serves 10

Oven: moderately hot, 200°C/400°F/Gas 6

1.1 kg (2½ lb) small new Jersey potatoes, washed with skin	Dry thoroughly on a cloth.
50 ml (2 fl oz) olive oil	Heat in a suitable pan in the preheated oven. It should be very hot.
salt and freshly ground pepper	Add the potatoes to the hot pan, and season. Roast until light brown in colour, about 7–10 minutes. Remove the potatoes with a perforated spoon, drain on kitchen paper and keep warm in a suitable dish. Pour the oil from the pan.
450 g (1 lb) mixed wild mushrooms, quickly washed and well drained	Add to the pan, and sauté quickly on top of the stove for about 2–3 minutes. Drain and season to taste, then add to the potato dish and toss together.
30 ml (2 tbsp) finely chopped parsley	Sprinkle over the potatoes and mushrooms, and serve.

Ceps   Chanterelles   Oyster   Morel

RATATOUILLE EN PÂTE FILO

These 'pouches' look spectacular for a special dinner party, and they're not difficult to make. They also make very good starters: serve them in a pool of smooth tomato sauce (see page 198).

Makes 20

Oven: moderate, 180°C/350°F/Gas 4

about **200 g** (7 oz) filo pastry (see page 202)	Roll out thinly. You want 10 sheets approximately 30 cm (12 in) square. Cut two sheets at a time into quarters (for 15 cm/6 in squares). You'll need 20 two-layer squares to serve two pouches per person.
about **675 g** (1½ lb) ratatouille, cut small (see page 152)	Place a tablespoonful in the middle of each double square, then gather up the ends into a pouch shape.
2 egg yolks, beaten with a little salt	Twist the top carefully to seal, using a little of the egg glaze if the pastry is not moist enough to cling to itself.
several outer leek leaves, blanched	Cut into 'strings', and use a couple to 'tie' each pouch. Fan the filo out at the top as much as you can. Brush all over with the egg glaze and place on a non-stick baking sheet (use a little oil on other sheets). Bake in the preheated oven for 10–12 minutes until golden brown.

TIP
Work as quickly as possible with the filo. Cover the filo not being used with a slightly damp cloth to prevent it from drying out.

TIP
When in season, many wild mushrooms are now quite commonly available, and their flavour is incomparable. Many can also be bought dried, and they retain almost as good a flavour; they need to be soaked in warm water to reconstitute them and carefully drained of grit (try to use the strained soaking water, it will have absorbed some of the mushrooms' fragrance). *Morels*, fresh in late spring, are small, dark and wrinkled like a prune; fresh *ceps* or *boletus edulis* are large, meaty and earthy, and are available in late summer and autumn; they are also dried, especially as the Italian *funghi porcini*. *Chanterelles* and *girolles*, both golden, spindly and fragrant, are available fresh (in the autumn) and dried. Other mushrooms, now cultivated, are *oyster* (oyster shaped, and full of flavour, much more so than the common cultivated field mushroom), and *shi'itake*, a Japanese mushroom cultivated on trees, and available fresh as well as dried.

SELECTION OF CHEESES

I like to serve a small selection of freshly cut cheeses after the main course. On this particular occasion I chose two English cheeses, and an unusual Swiss one. The mature Farmhouse Cheddar and the Stilton were in prime condition. The Cheddar should be smooth, slightly crumbly and yellowish in colour, with a full, rich and nutty flavour; it should always be freshly cut into wedges from the round. The Stilton should have a wrinkled brown/grey skin and blue-green veins radiating from the centre; there can be a little brown discoloration near the crust.

Tête de Moine (monk's head) is a Swiss cheese, made in large rounds, which is occasionally available in this country at specialist cheese shops. It used to be prepared by monks in the French part of Switzerland. (Sbrinz is an acceptable alternative.) The cheese gets its name from its look once it is prepared. A whole cheese comes covered in a rind, and before cutting, the rind must be sliced off the top and off about a third around the sides – it now looks like the head of a tonsured monk. A special cutter is then placed in the middle of the cheese and turned to shave off a paper-thin circular layer of cheese, which curls up like a frilled fan on the serving plate. Dust it with paprika.

Garnish the plate of cheeses with a small bunch of black grapes, and serve with slices of warm walnut and raisin bread (see page 22).

SYMPHONIE DE SORBET

Sorbets can be served in between courses, as a main dessert, or as here, just before the actual dessert, to freshen the palate.

Fresh fruit sorbets are very popular, and they are quite light to eat, especially those without egg white and a lot of alcohol (for a few *ice-cream* recipes, see pages 88–9). To taste them at their best, however, they should be freshly made, otherwise the fruit aroma is lost. Choose fruits for sorbets according to season (the following recipes can be adapted for other fruits), and they must be at their prime.

To make sorbets richer and slightly more substantial, they may be accompanied by fresh fruit of the season, and/or by a good home-made biscuit (see the Délices des Dames on page 188). A nice idea is to offer a *selection* of different sorbets – I chose five – with a little fruit to decorate. Try to have these in different colours so that the finished plate looks really attractive. Form into ovals by shaping sorbet into coquilles between two dessertspoons dipped in hot water, then arrange like spokes of a wheel on a plate, fruit between and in the middle. I serve this on black plates, with mint leaves to decorate and a sprinkling of icing sugar.

All the following sorbets serve four people, or can be formed into ten coquilles.

LEMON SORBET

150 g (5 oz) caster sugar 250 ml (9 fl oz) water	Dissolve sugar in water, then cool.
250 ml (9 fl oz) freshly squeezed lemon juice	Add, then pass through a fine sieve into a container. Freeze, whisking the ice vigorously from time to time, or transfer to a sorbetière and churn until smooth.

RHUBARB SORBET

400 g (14 oz) young rhubarb, well trimmed and washed	Cut into 5 cm (2 in) lengths, and put in a pan.
150 g (5 oz) caster sugar 100 ml (4 fl oz) water ½ lemon, juiced	Add, and simmer, covered, until rhubarb is soft, about 5–10 minutes. Cool. Freeze, whisking the ice vigorously from time to time, or transfer to a sorbetière and churn until smooth.

RASPBERRY SORBET

350 g (12 oz) raspberries	Liquidise and pass through a fine sieve.
100 g (4 oz) caster sugar **100 ml** (4 fl oz) water	Dissolve sugar in water over heat, cool, then add to the raspberry purée.
½ lemon, juiced	Stir in well, then pour into a container. Freeze, whisking the ice vigorously from time to time, or transfer to a sorbetière and churn until smooth.

MANGO SORBET

100 g (4 oz) caster sugar **100 g** (4 fl oz) water	Dissolve sugar in water then cool.
250 ml (9 fl oz) mango purée (see page 84) **2 g** (about ½ tsp) finely grated fresh ginger	Add to syrup, then liquidise and pass through a fine sieve.
1 lemon, juiced	Mix in, and leave to cool. Pour into a container and freeze, whisking the ice from time to time, or transfer to a sorbetière and churn until smooth and creamy.

TIP
Use only very ripe mangoes for this purée; even medium-ripe mangoes would be too hard to purée, and would lack the necessary sweetness.

KIWI FRUIT SORBET

400 g (14 oz) fully ripe kiwi fruit	Peel, remove cores, and liquidise flesh carefully to a purée, without crushing the seeds. Strain and discard the seeds.
50 ml (2 fl oz) water **100 ml** (4 fl oz) champagne **75 g** (3 oz) caster sugar	Boil together, and allow to cool. Add to the purée.
½ lemon, juiced a little Pernod (optional)	Add and mix in well, and transfer to a container. Freeze, whisking the ice vigorously from time to time, or transfer to a sorbetière and churn until a velvety consistency.

M

SOUFFLÉ AUX FRUITS DE LA PASSION

This soufflé rises like magic without the aid of flour – or a pump! The usual rule for soufflés applies – the guests must wait for the soufflé, and not the soufflé for the guests. For ten people, make *two* soufflés.

Serves 4–6

Oven: moderate, 180°C/350°F/Gas 4

melted butter and sugar for the dish	Butter a 1.5 litre (2½ pint) glass, china or silver soufflé dish evenly and carefully. Brush it on in two even layers, chilling well in between. Dust with sugar.
3 egg yolks **200 g** (7 oz) caster sugar **150 ml** (¼ pint) passion fruit juice (from 12–15 passion fruit, see Tip)	Beat the yolks with half the caster sugar and two-thirds of the passion fruit juice.
6 egg whites	Whisk the whites with the remaining caster sugar until thick and creamy, as for meringues. Very carefully fold the whites into the yolk mixture. Pour the mixture into the prepared dish, and give a fairly firm tap against the work surface to make it nice and smooth, with no air bubbles. Poach in a bain-marie on top of the stove, for 8–10 minutes. Remove from the bain-marie and bake in the preheated oven for 25–30 minutes.
20 g (¾ oz) caster sugar ½ lemon, juiced	To make the sauce, boil up the remaining passion fruit juice with the sugar and lemon juice.
10 ml (2 tsp) cornflour or arrowroot, slaked in a little water	Add just enough to thicken the sauce. Boil for 2–3 minutes only.
icing sugar for dusting	When the soufflé is ready, dust the top with icing sugar and serve immediately. Serve the sauce separately, alongside a little bowl of half-whipped cream.

TIP

The sweetest, most perfumed juice is found in the darkest and most wrinkled passion fruit – signs of ripeness. To make juice, scoop out seeds and flesh from the half 'shells', and place in a blender. Liquidise briefly to release the seeds from the juice, taking care not to break up the seeds. Strain into a measuring jug.

DÉLICES DES DAMES

Petits fours, the small sweet mouthfuls served after dinner with the coffee, fall into roughly three categories: the crisp little biscuits to which the name truly belongs (Carême said that these 'little ovens' were baked after the big cakes, when the oven was turned down); small iced fancy cakes; and items such as chocolate truffles, glacé and marzipan fruits which belong more in the realm of confectionery.

Palmiers, sesame biscuits and tuiles are delicious after dinner, when people like something to nibble on, but they are also useful in other ways. All three could serve as coffee or tea accompaniments at other times of the day, and go well with ice-creams and sorbets. The tuiles could be made bigger and shaped over the greased bottom of a bowl for a basket shape to hold a selection of fruit for a dessert.

For all three *petits fours* recipes, use either non-stick, heavy baking sheets, or line ordinary baking sheets with silicone or parchment paper brushed with about 15 ml (1 tbsp) vegetable oil.

SESAME BISCUITS

Makes 24 biscuits	Oven: moderate, 180°C/350°F/Gas 4
1 egg **40 g** (1½ oz) caster sugar	Whisk together in a bowl until frothy.
20 g (¾ oz) butter, melted **40 g** (1½ oz) wholewheat flour **40 g** (1½ oz) plain white flour **75 g** (3 oz) sesame seeds ½ lemon, finely zested	Stir in, and mix to a firm dough.
a little milk	Add if necessary.
flour for dusting	Roll dough as thinly as possible on a lightly floured board. Using a 6 cm (2½ in) cutter, cut out as many rounds as you can. Transfer these with a palette knife to a prepared baking sheet, and bake in the preheated oven for about 15 minutes until golden. Leave to cool and firm up for a few moments on the baking sheet before transferring to a cooling rack. Leave until completely cold before storing in an airtight tin.

TUILES

Makes 8–10

Oven: moderate, 180°C/350°F/Gas 4

3 large, very fresh egg whites **100 g** (4 oz) icing sugar, sifted a pinch of salt	Whisk the whites a little, then add the sugar and salt. Beat in thoroughly.
15 g (½ oz) unsalted butter, melted **100 g** (4 oz) plain flour, sifted	Add gradually to the mixture, and mix well.
1½ oranges, finely zested	Fold in lightly. Allow to rest for 2 hours. With your fingers, spread the mixture into eight or ten circles of approximately 9 cm (3½ in) on the prepared baking sheets (use a little of the mixture to anchor the paper to the sheet). You don't need to have perfect circles. Allow room for spreading during cooking.
25 g (1 oz) flaked almonds	Sprinkle over the top, and bake in the preheated oven for about 6–8 minutes until golden.
15 ml (1 tbsp) vegetable oil	Lightly oil the sides of a couple of clean bottles. Remove the tuiles from the oven, then from the baking sheets, and place each circle over the bottles so that they droop into a semi-circular shape. Leave until cold and firm, then store in an airtight tin.

TIP

The secret of successful tuiles is to work quickly and give yourself plenty of space. They need little cooking, and must be watched *very* carefully. When they come out of the oven, allow to firm very briefly (otherwise they break), then remove from the tray. At this moment the tuiles are still supple enough to be moulded. Drape immediately over the bottle, rolling pin or pudding bowl, otherwise they harden on the tray.

PALMIERS

Makes about 20

about **13 oz** (375 g) puff
  pastry (see page 201)
50 g (2 oz) caster (or
  vanilla) sugar, sifted

Oven: hot, 220°C/425°F/Gas 7

Dust the work surface with some of the sugar, then roll
the pastry out thinly into a rectangle roughly 35 × 19 cm
(14 × 7½ in). Trim edges.

Fold in half lengthwise, to mark the middle, then open up
again. By eye, divide each half roughly into three (see
illustrations).

Brush the whole of the top of the rectangle with water and
sprinkle with sugar. As you begin to fold, brush each *new*
surface with water and sprinkle with sugar.

Fold in the first third at each end, then fold that fold over
again so that both first folded edges are at the middle. Fold
over finally so that there are six layers of pastry.

Do *not* brush water and sugar on the final surface.

Leave to rest, lightly covered with clingfilm, for at least an
hour in a cool place. Chill for 10 minutes.

With the final fold to the top, cut the pastry into 1 cm
(½ in) wide slices with a sharp knife. Arrange on the
prepared baking sheets, keeping them well apart (they
double in size during cooking). Tweak the rounded tips
outwards gently.

Bake in the preheated oven for 15–20 minutes, turning
them over halfway through, and dusting with sugar, or
until golden, crisp and dry.

Cool on a rack.

Folding and cutting palmiers.

From left to right: Palmiers
(opposite); Tuiles (page 189);
Mosimann's Special Chocolate
Truffles

BASIC RECIPES

In this section I have gathered together the recipes that recur throughout the book in some form or another. The stocks are vital for soups and many sauces: the ones selected are 'light' or 'white', but for a darker, brown stock, whether poultry or meat, you can roast the bones first in a hot oven (as for the beef bones for gravy on page 43), before simmering.

Here too are the herb mixtures I created to cut down on the salt content of recipes, as well as several basic sauces. There's a home-made yoghurt recipe on page 4, but there are also several home-made fresh cheese recipes which are very useful in many aspects of cookery. Pastries – particularly filo – are used in many recipes, as well as multicoloured home-made noodles. Finally, I have written some notes about the oils and vinegars I like best, with hints about how to 'enrich' them at home.

VEGETABLE STOCK

Choose your vegetables according to season and availability. Don't throw them away after they have flavoured the stock – stir into rice, or purée them as a vegetable mousseline or the basis of a soup. This stock is usually used for soups, sauces and vegetarian dishes. It can be reduced and used in sauces like tomato, and in salad dressings instead of oil if you're following a healthy Cuisine Naturelle diet. The oil below can be omitted, of course, but you need to use a non-stick pan when sweating the vegetables.

Makes 2 litres (3½ pints)

100 g (4 oz) onions, peeled **100 g** (4 oz) leeks, washed and trimmed **100 g** (4 oz) carrots, trimmed **75 g** (3 oz) cabbage or cauliflower, washed **75 g** (3 oz) fennel, trimmed **75 g** (3 oz) tomatoes with skins	Chop all vegetables finely, keeping them separate.
a little vegetable or herbed olive oil	Gently sauté the onion and leek in the oil in a large stock pot for 4–5 minutes. Add the remaining vegetables and sauté for a further 10 minutes.

10 ml (2 tsp) fennel seeds 4 parsley stalks 1 strip lemon peel 1 bay leaf 1 clove 4 peppercorns 3 sprigs tarragon 1 leek leaf	Meanwhile, tie herbs and spices with string into the leek leaf for a bouquet garni.
3 litres (5¼ pints) water	Add to the pot with the bouquet garni, bring to the boil, and simmer for 20 minutes. Strain through a cloth or fine sieve, allowing it to drip.
salt and freshly ground pepper	Season to taste.

WHITE POULTRY STOCK

This clear, mild stock is used for poaching chicken, and for chicken and other soups and sauces. The flesh of the boiling fowl can be used afterwards for various cold dishes such as salads, sandwiches, mousses, etc.

Makes 1 litre (1¾ pints)

1 boiling fowl or 1 kg (2¼ lb) chicken carcass and bones	Place in a large saucepan, pour over boiling water, then bring back to the boil. Boil for about 2 minutes, then drain and rinse.
approx **2 litres** (3½ pints) water	Pour over chicken or bones, bring to the boil and skim.
50 g (2 oz) white bouquet garni (onion, white of leek, celeriac and herbs, tied together)	Add, and leave to simmer gently for 2 hours, occasionally skimming to remove the fat from the top. Remove the chicken or bones. Strain the stock through a fine sieve or a cloth, allowing it to drip.
salt and freshly ground pepper	Season to taste, and chill. Remove any surface fat.

TIP

Boiling fowl are older, tougher birds of about ten to twelve months, which weigh up to 3 kg (6½ lb). They are often egg-layers past their best, but are full of flavour. There is quite a lot of fat in the vent of boiling fowl; remove this carefully before poaching the bird. They are no longer to be seen as much as they once were. If your butcher can't oblige, try a fishmonger.

BROWN LAMB STOCK

Use beef bones instead to make a brown beef stock. Ask the butcher to chop the bones for you.

Makes 1 litre (1¾ pints)	Oven: very hot, 240°C/475°F/Gas 9
1 kg (2¼ lb) raw lamb bones, chopped into small pieces	Place in a roasting tin and brown on all sides for about 20 minutes. Drain of all fat, and place bones in a large pan.
50 g (2 oz) diced onion, carrot, celeriac and herbs	Place in roasting tin and roast carefully for a further 4–5 minutes. Add to the bones.
approx **2 litres** (3½ pints) cold water	Use a little to deglaze the roasting tin, then add all the water to the pan. Bring to the boil and skim. Allow to simmer for about 2 hours, occasionally removing the fat by skimming. Strain the stock through a fine sieve or cloth, allowing it to drip.
salt and freshly ground pepper	Season to taste, and chill.

TIP
Lamb can be quite fatty, so it is often a good idea to let the stock cool, then chill it so that any fat can set on the top of the stock. This is then easily lifted off with a spoon.

FISH STOCK

A good fish stock should only be made from the bones and trimmings of white fish such as plaice, whiting, turbot, halibut or sole (oily fish will not do). Simmer the fish bones – cut up to extract more flavour – for about 20 minutes only, as a longer cooking time can make the stock gluey. Depending on whether you are adhering to Cuisine Naturelle principles, you can omit the oil and wine. Reduce the stock if you like, to concentrate the flavour. Keep for a day only in the refrigerator, or freeze.

Makes 1.2 litres (a good 2 pints)

1 kg (2¼ lb) white fish bones and trimmings, broken up	Wash thoroughly and blanch if necessary (see below).
15 ml (1 tbsp) olive oil **50 g** (2 oz) vegetable dice (onion, carrot, celeriac and white of leek)	Heat the oil gently in a suitable pan, then add the onion and carrot and cook to soften but not colour, about 1 minute. Add the celeriac and leek and sweat for a further minute. Add the fish bones and trimmings and sweat for a few minutes.
100 ml (4 fl oz) dry white wine **1.2 litres** (a good 2 pints) water a little salt a few white peppercorns, crushed	Add, and bring to the boil.
30 g (1¼ oz) white mushrooms or trimmings (optional) a few sprigs of dill and basil (or parsley)	Add, and simmer very gently for 15 minutes, a maximum of 20 minutes. Strain through a sieve lined with a cloth or muslin, allowing the liquid to drip through slowly.
lemon juice	Season to taste with salt, pepper and lemon juice.

TIP
For the clearest stock, the bones must be very fresh, and all gills, viscera, etc, must be removed. If they're not completely fresh, blanch them. Pour over hot water, bring to the boil, then strain and cool in cold water.

COURT BOUILLON

Fish can be poached or shellfish cooked in this mild flavoured stock, but it can also be used as the steaming medium *beneath* fish. It can be made according to Cuisine Naturelle principles, without the wine. It can be frozen, but is best used straightaway. Other ingredients can be added to vary the flavour – a good vinegar instead of or as well as the wine, for instance, when steaming as on page 94.

Makes 2.5 litres (4¼ pints)

500 ml (18 fl oz) dry white wine (optional) **2 litres** (3½ pints) water	In a large saucepan, bring to the boil.
200 g (7 oz) carrots, peeled and diced **100 g** (4 oz) white of leek, cut into rings **100 g** (4 oz) onions, sliced **50 g** (2 oz) celery, sliced **1** clove garlic, with skin **5** sprigs parsley **1** small sprig thyme **½** bay leaf **5** white peppercorns, crushed **3** coriander seeds	Add, and allow to simmer for 10 minutes.
salt	Season to taste, and then strain through a fine sieve.

HERB MIXTURES

These herb mixtures were created to cut down on the use of salt in Cuisine Naturelle recipes, but they can be used successfully in many other recipes. The proportions have been very carefully worked out so that the flavours of the herbs do not overpower the dish in which they are used. Fresh herbs only must be used, of course (although mixtures can be frozen), and using a pinch (or more) in individual recipes will reduce the need for salt by 50 per cent.

For fish and shellfish
10 ml (2 tsp) finely cut dill
5 ml (1 tsp) finely chopped thyme
5 ml (1 tsp) finely cut basil
5 ml (1 tsp) plucked chervil leaves
2.5 ml (½ tsp) plucked coriander leaves
2.5 ml (½ tsp) finely cut tarragon

For meat and poultry
10 ml (2 tsp) finely chopped thyme
7.5 ml (1½ tsp) finely chopped marjoram
5 ml (1 tsp) finely chopped rosemary
2.5 ml (½ tsp) finely chopped oregano
5 ml (1 tsp) finely cut basil
1.25 ml (¼ tsp) finely cut sage

For vegetables
5 ml (1 tsp) finely chopped oregano
5 ml (1 tsp) finely cut dill
5 ml (1 tsp) plucked chervil leaves
5 ml (1 tsp) finely cut borage

TIP
When cutting herbs, here and throughout the book, each should be cut in a different way. Tougher herb leaves, like thyme and rosemary, can actually be chopped in a rapid movement with a large cook's knife or a herb chopper; more tender leaves, such as chives, dill or basil, must be deliberately cut in individual cutting movements. The leaves of coriander or chervil should be individually picked or plucked from the stem.

TOMATO CONCASSE

This basic sauce has very few calories, is very light and colourful, and has a good flavour which goes well with both fish and meat. The lovely coral colour forms a welcome contrast with other vegetables, whether used as garnish or sauce.

Serves 4

50 ml (2 fl oz) olive oil **20 g** (¾ oz) shallot, finely chopped **1** clove garlic, unpeeled	Sweat together without colouring in a pan.
1 kg (2¼ lb) ripe tomatoes, skinned and seeded (see page 124)	Chop into small pieces.
a few sprigs of oregano and thyme salt and freshly ground pepper	Add, with the tomatoes, and season to taste. Cover and cook carefully for about 15 minutes until soft and all the liquid has evaporated. Remove the garlic clove and herbs and, if necessary, season again with salt and pepper.

TIP
Tomatoes for use in a recipe such as this must always be seeded as, quite apart from the smoother texture, the seeds may be green, unripe and bitter in flavour. Some finely cut basil could be added to the sauce at the end.

TOMATO SAUCE

The colour and flavour of this sauce depends on bright red, ripe tomatoes; to guarantee ripeness, buy them a few days in advance.

Serves 4

2 small shallots, finely chopped ½ clove garlic, crushed **20 g** (¾ oz) butter	Sauté the vegetables in the butter for 3–4 minutes until transparent.
1 sprig thyme **1** sprig rosemary	Add, and sauté very gently for 1 minute more.
1 kg (2¼ lb) firm, ripe tomatoes, skinned, seeded and chopped (see page 124)	Add, and simmer for 10–12 minutes. Remove the herbs and purée the sauce in a blender. Return the sauce to the pan and bring to the boil.
salt, freshly ground pepper and a little sugar	Season to taste.

WHITE WINE SAUCE

This sauce may be used as the base for quite a few variations. Always use the stock appropriate to the dish the sauce will accompany – for example, fish stock for fish. A squeeze of lemon or lime juice added at the end will often balance the sauce perfectly.

Serves 4

400 ml (14 fl oz) fish stock (see page 195) **100 ml** (4 fl oz) dry white wine **50 ml** (2 fl oz) Noilly Prat **1** small shallot, finely chopped	Combine in a shallow saucepan, and reduce by half by fast boiling.
150 ml (¼ pint) double cream	Add, and simmer gently to reduce the sauce until it coats a spoon.
50 g (2 oz) butter, chilled and cut into cubes (optional)	Remove the pan from the heat and whisk butter in, one cube at a time. Strain the sauce through a fine sieve or muslin, and bring back to the boil.
salt and freshly ground pepper	Season to taste and serve.

Variation

Parsley Sauce

Make a white wine sauce, and mix in 30 ml (2 tbsp) finely chopped parsley. Liquidise with a stick blender to make a smooth and lovely green sauce.

FROMAGE BLANC

This basic 'junket' cheese contains virtually no fat. It is made in the same way as cream cheese, but using skimmed milk instead of single cream or full-fat milk. It is very useful in a great number of recipes, particularly those which adhere to Cuisine Naturelle principles – in home-made sausages, in bread, in little leek parcels, in dressings etc.

Makes about 600 g (1 lb 5 oz)

1 litre (1¾ pints) skimmed milk	Place in a very clean saucepan and heat to 43°C/110°F (use a thermometer). Remove from heat, and rest for a few moments.
¼ junket tablet	Dissolve in the warm milk. Stir well, cover, and allow to stand for 24 hours at room temperature until set. Line a colander with muslin or cheesecloth and suspend over a large bowl or container (the bottom of the colander must not touch the bottom of the container). Place the set junket in the cloth and let the whey drain out for about 45–60 minutes. Do not touch the cloth. Remove from the cloth and place in a suitable container. It is ready for use immediately, but can be kept in the refrigerator for up to 2 days.

QUARK

This is a simple curd cheese. It originated in Germany, but now can be found in many other countries.

Makes about 300 ml (½ pint)

1 litre (1¾ pints) skimmed milk	Bring just to the boil.
½ lemon, juiced	Add, remove pan from the heat, and leave to settle for a while. Bring to the boil again, then let the milk cool once more. It will have curdled. Place in a cloth-lined colander over a bowl and leave to drain as for fromage blanc above. Remove from cloth, and cool in the refrigerator before use.

Variation

Yoghurt Curd Cheese	A similar cheese can be made, in exactly the same way, with fresh home-made yoghurt (see page 4). Drain for about 6 hours then chill and use as soon as possible.

PUFF PASTRY

Many people are put off making puff pastry because it takes so long. This version is a little easier and quicker.

Makes about 1 kg (2¼ lb)

450 g (1 lb) strong plain white flour a good pinch of salt	Sift into a large bowl.
350 g (12 oz) butter, chilled	Cut into nut-sized cubes, and mix into the flour, coating all the cubes.
175 ml (6 fl oz) cold water	Add, and mix with a palette knife. Knead to a dough quickly but keeping the cubes of butter fairly whole. Leave to rest for at least 5 minutes (preferably 30), covered with clingfilm. On a lightly floured board roll out to a long rectangle of about 2 cm (¾ in) thick. Fold the two long ends of the dough evenly towards the centre so that they meet in the middle. Then fold over both halves of the dough so that the middle now becomes one of the sides. This is one double turn. Wrap carefully again and chill for a few minutes (preferably for about 20). Bring the pastry out and lay on the lightly floured board with the last fold to your right, and roll out to a long rectangle again. Repeat the double turn and chilling three more times (for four double turns in all), then rest the pastry for at least an hour before use.

TIP

Roll in only one direction – straight in front of you – and use quick and light movements. If you roll too hard the pastry will be uneven, and the butter may be pushed out from between the layers.

FILO PASTRY

This pastry – which is the only one used in Cuisine Naturelle recipes – is here made without oil or butter. Only a very small proportion of fat – usually oil – is used in the making of true filo pastry; which is why it is so 'short', and why some cooks brush layers of the pastry with oil or melted butter in their recipes. The pastry must be rolled extremely thinly, and when baked it is very crisp and light.

Makes 650 g (1¼–1½ lb)

300 g (11 oz) strong white bread flour 100 g (4 oz) cornflour 2.5 ml (½ tsp) salt	Sieve together into a bowl, and make a well in the centre.
250 ml (9 fl oz) water	Pour about half into the well, and gradually draw the flour into the water, mixing smoothly and evenly. Add the remaining water and knead until the dough is smooth and does not stick to the hands. Cover with a damp cloth and leave to rest for 1–2 hours in a cool place. This allows the dough to develop its elasticity fully. Divide the dough into quarters and cover the pieces not being rolled with an upturned hot bowl (to keep it warm and pliable). Start rolling one piece out on a floured surface, gradually making the sheet thinner and thinner. (Many advise testing a piece over a clean patterned cloth; when you see the pattern through the paste, it is thin enough.) When the dough sheet becomes too large and unwieldy, cut in half and continue to roll. When as thin as it is possible to roll, place the sheet over the back of the hand, and pull gently down from the edges to stretch even more. Work carefully so that it does not break. Roll the other pieces of dough in the same way, and cover dough and sheets at all times with plastic or clingfilm. Use sheets as quickly as possible.

HOME-MADE EGG NOODLES

Noodles are fairly simple to make at home, and taste very much better than the bought variety. They're good with fish and chicken, and excellent in salads. Always cook them *al dente* in plenty of water, and drain very well.

Serves 4

200 g (7 oz) strong plain white flour (or fine wholewheat flour), sieved **25 g** (1 oz) fine wheat semolina	Mix together in a large bowl and make a well in the centre.
7.5 ml (½ tbsp) olive oil **1** egg a pinch of salt **45–60 ml** (3–4 tbsp) hot water	Place the remaining ingredients in the well. Gradually work the flour and semolina in towards the middle and knead into a very firm, smooth dough. (You may need a little extra flour.) Wrap in a damp cloth, and allow to rest in a cool place for at least 2–3 hours. Divide the dough into five pieces and roll out each as thinly as possible, stretching gently as you roll. Do this as quickly as you can, too – no more than 8 minutes – otherwise it will dry, lose its elasticity and become impossible to roll thinly. Leave to firm up for a few minutes (or for longer, until becoming leathery, but still pliable enough to fold) before cutting into noodles. To cut, lay a couple of pieces on top of each other, fold up into a flat roll, and cut into strips approximately 6 mm (¼ in) wide. Curl into nests. Cook immediately while still fairly fresh, or leave to dry further. Boil fresh for 2–3 minutes, for about double that time if dried, but always test to see if cooked *al dente*, with a little 'bite' remaining.

Variations

Saffron Noodles

Make exactly as above, but dissolve a large pinch of saffron threads in the hot water first before proceeding.

Spinach Noodles

Make exactly as above, but add 100 g (4 oz) squeezed-dry spinach purée instead of the hot water (adding a little warm water if necessary).

Tomato Noodles

Make exactly as above, but add 50 g (2 oz) tomato purée instead of the hot water.

Oils

Oils are one of the oldest ingredients in history: the Ancient Egyptians apparently made it from radishes! Many national cuisines are today characterised by the oil made from the dominant oil-producing plant – Mediterranean cuisines by olive, Far Eastern by sesame, Caribbean and West African by palm, and Indonesian by peanut, for instance.

My own favourite for cooking is cold pressed extra virgin olive oil from Italy, which is a wonderful dark green colour. This is the pressed, pure, first 'juice' of the olives, which has had no heat applied to it. Spanish oil is almost as good, while the French, some of which is second pressing, although good, does not have such a full flavour. I use olive oil instead of butter in a lot of my cooking as it is healthier, containing more polyunsaturates. It is also a favourite in salad dressings. At home I often 'enrich' my own olive oil with herbs and other flavourings, and I give a few ideas below.

Other oils that I like are hazelnut and walnut, both of which are cold pressed from the respective nuts. They're both strong and rather expensive, but go a long way as they should be diluted with a lighter and blander oil for use in a dressing. Nut oil dressings are delicious with fresh green leaves straight from the garden, particularly hazelnut with red wine vinegar. Keep both oils in the refrigerator.

Bland and light oils to use in cooking are sunflower, groundnut (peanut), grapeseed and safflower. The latter two are useful in low-cholesterol diets as they are high in poly-unsaturates.

Other less usual oils available are almond, avocado, coco-nut, mustard and sesame. These are expensive, but each has its use in particular styles of cookery.

Everyone interested in cooking should have a selection of oils – one good olive as a basic, a safflower or groundnut oil for general use, and one or two specialist oils, such as walnut for the occasional accent, and sesame for oriental cookery.

Flavoured Oils

Your own herb oils are extremely simple to make at home, and they look and smell as delicious as they taste. Simply wash and dry the herbs well then use in the rough proportion of about 30 ml (2 tbsp) crushed herb per 300 ml (½ pint) oil. You can use a mixture – thyme and garlic, for example, is good to brush on foods on the barbecue – or just one. Leave in a cool dark place in a cork- or plastic-topped glass bottle for at least 10 days before using, giving the bottle a shake every now and again.

You could make rosemary or basil oils (both are good for salad dressings, and basil is best preserved in oil anyway), fennel, tarragon, sage or bay. Use olive oil for the best flavour, but you could also use sunflower, safflower, grapeseed or groundnut oils as a base.

After the 10 days, check to see if the flavour is pronounced enough, or to your taste. For decorative (and further flavouring purposes), you could strain the oil of the crushed herbs and replace in the glass bottle with a sprig of the whole herb.

For a delicious 'double-enriched' olive oil, use some oil-cured Italian olives (and a few dried red chillies or crushed garlic cloves as well if you like), as above.

Vinegars

Vinegar has been known as long as wine or ale, as it actually consists of alcohol that has been soured by the action of bacteria (thus *vin aigre*, sour wine). I quite often make my own vinegar with a leftover quarter bottle of wine; I add either some mother of vinegar (the old-fashioned 'starter' required) or a little vinegar to increase acidity; it only takes a few days.

There are various types of vinegar available for use in cooking. The ones I like are the wine vinegars, red and white; these are made in wine-growing countries, and the best are produced by the slow Orléans method, which preserves the flavour of the wine. Sherry vinegar is good too: it has a warm, rounded acidity, and is ideal for light salads. In China and Japan, rice vinegar is made from rice wine, and cider vinegar is made in countries with an apple-growing tradition (this is said to be very healthy). My favourite, though, is balsamic, an Italian wine vinegar matured in wood, sometimes for up to 50 years, which has a quite unique sweetness and lightness. Malt and distilled vinegars are made in countries with a beer tradition from unhopped ale; these should not be used in dressings or cooking as they are very strong and acid, but are useful in preserving (and lots of people like them sprinkled over their fish and chips).

Flavoured Vinegars

As with oils, vinegars can be flavoured at home too, with fruit, vegetables and herbs. Raspberry vinegar has been very popular in recent years (if a little *mis*-used on occasions), and it is simply made. Steep 450 g (1 lb) slightly bruised raspberries (or you can use any soft fruit) in 600 ml (1 pint) white wine vinegar for about 4 days, covered with a cloth. Stir occasionally, then strain through muslin into a pan. Add 100 g (4 oz) sugar (or to taste) to each 600 ml (1 pint) of liquid, bring to the boil and boil for about 10 minutes. Cool and bottle.

Herb vinegars are even easier. Simply pick the herbs before they flower, wash then bruise them slightly, and place in a large jar. Use a good 45 ml (3 tbsp) herb to 1 litre (1¾ pints) vinegar. Cover with vinegar, seal tightly (with cork or plastic, never metal), and leave in a dark place for at least 6 weeks. Strain through muslin and re-bottle, adding a fresh sprig of the herb for a final decorative touch.

Use cider or wine vinegar for herbs: red for garlic (about

75 g/3 oz chopped cloves); white for tarragon, basil, fennel, rosemary, thyme or mint (or try cider for the latter). Mixed herb vinegars are possible too, as are herb seed vinegars (45 ml/3 tbsp crushed coriander, dill or fennel seeds).

Index